40 Great Home Business Ideas For Baby Boomers

Easy to start home businesses that can make you a lot of money

David Rye

WESTERN PUBLICATIONS
10271 South 175th Avenue
Goodyear, AZ 85358-5502

Contents

Getting Started

If you keep searching, you will find the startup you're looking for

Boomers have learned a great deal during their careers and have developed expertise in more areas than many may realize. Their expertise can prove to be a valuable asset in creating the foundation of a home-based business. It might be in the area of computer software, accounting, education, writing, computer hardware, landscaping, desktop publishing, marketing, people management, or in many other business oriented fields. *40 Great Home Businesses Ideas For Baby Boomers* offers you several exciting opportunities to get started.

Review the startup options that are featured in the book and get creative in terms of thinking about what you would enjoy doing. Although starting up a home business may seem like a daunting task, it doesn't have to be. Yes, it will be challenging, but it can also be fun and can reward you financially beyond your wildest expectations.

Each of the forty business profiles are organized in a concise, informative way to help you quickly get a realistic perspective of the nature of the business, what it involves, and what it offers. As you review the startup profiles, you'll be able to weigh the pros and cons in relation to one another to help determine which one is best for you.

Each profile begins with a general description of the business and what likely career skills are helpful in supporting that business venture. At the end of each profile, you will find helpful books, organizations, associations, publications, training programs, and websites listed in a table that provide you with additional relevant information you may need to take the next step.

Marketing Your Startup

The selling process is the starting point for your home business. Nothing happens until you make your first sale. Because sales and marketing are so important to success in your business, we provide a list of what others have found to be the best methods of getting business in each profile. You may find this to be the most valuable information you get from this book because it's information you usually can learn only through actual experience, which can be both costly and time consuming. Use this section to determine how you will identify your target prospects and how you'll reach them through advertising and promotional programs.

What to Charge

Just how important is selecting the right price for what you're selling? It could mean the difference between staying in business and going out of business. The fact is that too high a price can kill your business, as can too low a price. Finding that magic number requires careful thought and planning, which is why the subject is covered in each profile. The price of a product or service tells consumers what kind of value and quality to expect before they buy it. Establishing a price for a product isn't easy, and in many cases, pricing a service is even harder still.

Knowing the ranges of what one can charge is always a tricky question for many home businesses, yet without this information it's hard to make realistic decisions about starting a particular business. This section provides price ranges from across the country, tips for how prices are typically structured, and common variations in fees among various niches and specialties in the field. All our pricing data are based on inputs from experts in that field. It's important to note, however, that there is always variation in pricing from region to region and sometimes even within a metropolitan area.

Financial Projections

This section summarizes pertinent financial considerations with each startup. You are encouraged to prepare financial projections for any startup you are considering. Financial projection templates are included in the Appendix to help make it a relatively easy task. The following is a summary of the financial projections and associated templates that are included in the Appendix:

- **Funding requirement template** is used to determine how much money is needed to start the business and how will the money be used.

- **Income statement template** is used to determine how much you must sell to cover all costs and make a profit.

- **Cash flow template** is used to determine how money will flow into your business in the form of revenues and flow out of the business to cover expenses on a monthly basis.

- **Balance sheet template** is used to determine the cash value of your assets and liabilities. The purpose of the balance sheet is to paint a picture of what your business is worth.

Comparing Startup Options

To help you compare different startup options that you may be considering, answer the questions in the Business Startup Questionnaire for each startup that you are considering. It will help you determine the viability of one startup option against another.

BUSSINESS STARTUP QUESTIONNAIRE		
The type of business that I want to start is:		
Business Type Questions	**Yes**	**No**
Is this a business that you can get excited about?		
Am I in a suitable location for this business?		
Do I have the financial resources to start this business?		
Will this business generate the income that I need?		
Am I physically and mentally healthy enough to run this business?		
Will operating this business help me reach my goals?		
Do I need any special certificates or licenses to run this business?		
Will I enjoy running this business now and five years from now?		
Special Skills and Knowledge Questions	**High**	**Low**
How would you rate your expertise to run this type of business?		
Do I have any special skills that can be applied to this business?		
How would you rate your decision making abilities?		
How would you rate your financial and budging skills?		
How would you rate your money		

management skills?		
How would you rate your goal setting and planning skills?		
How would you rate your networking and direct sales skills?		

Putting It All Together

Owning and operating a business is like a balancing act at the circus. You often have to make personal and financial compromises to get the business up and running successfully. As with anything in life that is worthwhile, you must make sacrifices along the way to build a successful home business. However, if the sacrifices cause you to lose focus on the business that you started, chances are you will be miserable and the business will ultimately fail.

Before you start out, consider all factors and take your time to evaluate all of the variables in the business planning process. We feel confident that this book will open your eyes to the many startup possibilities that are available to you. It provides you with access to the information and tools you need to pursue them. Sources for additional information are summarized as follows:

Associations

U.S. Small Business Administration (800) 827-5722; *sba.gov*

American Home Business Association (866) 396-7773 homebusinessworks.com

Books & Publications

The Best Home Businesses for the 21st Century by Paul and Sarah Edwards

You Can Make Money from Your Hobby: Building a Business Doing What You Love by Lilly Walters and Martha Campbell

Entrepreneur's Ultimate Start-Up Directory: 1500 Great Business Ideas! by *James* Stephenson

Websites

Boconline.com list hundreds of business opportunity classified ads online.

Entrepreneur.com is an online small business resource center providing information and advice on products, services and resources.

Home-based-business-opportunities.com features hundreds of home based and small business opportunities listings.

Homebusinessmag.com is an online magazine with information, advice, tools and links for home business owners.

Powerhomebiz.com provides information, advice and tools for home business owners.

Sbomag.com is the Small Business Opportunities Magazine providing readers with the latest small business opportunities news, information and industry resources.

Home Business Opportunities

Planning every aspect of your startup will be critical to its future success. It's a must if you are going to succeed. Ninety percent of people who did not conduct any meaningful planning when they started their home business went out of business in their first year of operation. The business planning process requires that you analyze each business opportunity, research and compile data, and make conclusions based mainly on what the facts reveal. There are several inexpensive personal computer programs that are available to help you get through the business planning process (see Quicken.com for an example).

Business planning also helps you define your goals and determine the steps you need to take to achieve them. The business plan that you create becomes a road map that takes you from point A to Z and a yardstick to measure the success of each goal you set within your plan. This is not to say that your plan must be chock full of deadlines, but the basics must be covered including marketing strategies, advertising and sales tactics, and financial objectives. The home business profiles that follow are setup to get you started in the planning process.

Accounting Services

The one thing that has remained constant from the time of ancient Babylonia is the need to have someone maintain the accounting records of their business transactions. There are a number of lucrative startup opportunities that are available to you in the business sector. While accounting software has reduced the need for many smaller businesses to have in-house accountants, it has given rise to a need for independent accountants who can do part-time accounting out of their home office. The demand for accountants will remain strong, particularly with small businesses.

If you have a background in accounting or finance, then accounting can be a good source of income for many years. Along with a good sense for number, many roles in a corporate accounting setting can serve as a background for an accounting service business. Use the information and ideas in the following sections to create a business plan for accounting services.

Business Overview

The demand for accountants will remain strong, particularly among firms with fewer than fifty employees. You'll need to decide upon the scope of your services you want to specialize in. Some accountants offer complete services; others stick to accounts receivable, accounts payable, auditing, or payroll. Some combine accounting with preparing tax returns for their clients. Points to cover in the company introduction part of your business plan are the identification of the types of accounting services you plan to offer. Then, clearly state your company's mission (25 words or less) and identify your key objectives.

Accounting Overview			
	Low	Medium	High
Cost to Start		*	
Overhead	*		
Potential earnings		*	
Computer skills			*
Deadline pressure		*	
Flexible hours		*	
Job stress		*	

Marketing Accounting Services

The key benefit you offer clients is providing a higher skill level than they can afford to get by hiring a full-time employee. By using your services they can spend more time serving customers and doing marketing, thus improving their focus and reducing their overall cost. Focusing on small businesses that cannot afford to have a full-time accountant on staff and are too busy doing business to do accounting themselves will guarantee you a steady flow of clients. You can target your accounting practice at law firms, medical practices, construction companies, or any other industry well represented in your area. The following list will give you some ideas on how to develop a marketing and sales base for an accounting services business:

- Networking face-to-face inside business and trade organizations such as the chamber of commerce and business referral organizations.

- Obtaining referrals and doing overload work for CPA firms, accounting firms, and financial planners.

- Get listed as a support service in referral services that professional associations maintain for their members.

- Have a website that identifies what services you offer so that potential customers using a search engine will find your site.

- Calling on retail stores and service firms within your market area and introduce yourself and your business.

- List your business in the Yellow Pages and your website in Web directories like *switchboard.com* and *anywho.com*. Consider placing ads on local directory sites like *Yahoo Get Local* and *SuperPages*.

What to Charge

How much should you charge will depend on the geographical area covered by your business? Most independent accountants charge by the hour with fees ranging between $25 and $75 an hour. Some charge below $25, and a few can command more than $75 an hour depending on locale and the industries they work in. Some charge by the job or by transaction (i.e., number of checks or invoices processed). If you're charging a flat weekly or monthly rate, be sure to have a letter of engagement that defines what you will be doing and when you will be charging for extra work.

Financial Projections

Apply the information in the following financial projection table will help you setup your own financial projections in the templates covered in the Appendix.

Accounting Services Business Financial Projections	
Funding Requirements	Projecting what you will expend starting up this business should be minimal if you already have the computer equipment you need. If not, include those costs in your

	funding requirements worksheet.
Income and Expenses	Projected total monthly revenue is subtracted from total monthly expenses to determine how much you plan to make.
Cash Flow	The cash flow projection shows how money will flow into your business in the form of revenues and flow out of the business in the form of expenses.
Assets and Liabilities	The balance sheet lists the cash value of your assets and liabilities. Total liabilities are subtracted from the total value of your assets to determine your net worth or equity position in your business.

Putting It All Together

The information sources in the table below will help you develop and finalize your business plan for an accounting services business. Sources for additional information are summarized as follows:

Associations

The American Institute of Professional Accountants; *www.aipb.com;* (800-622-0121) offers certification exam, training materials, and a telephone hot line that is open to nonmembers.

Books & Publications

Haw to Open Your Own In-Home Accounting Service by Julie Mucha. Available both in print and as an e-book: (619) 449-0675; *www.inhomeaccountanting.bizland.com*

Websites

The Sleeter Group trains in *QuickBooks & Publications* and *NetLedger* accounting software and maintains a database of accountants on its site: *www.sleeter.com;* (888) 484-5484.

The U.S. Department of Agriculture Graduate School offers distance learning courses in accounting: *http://grad.usda.gov;* (888) 744-4723.

Universal Accounting Center sells a video home-study accounting course; *www.universalaccounting.com:* *(800)*343-4827. The company provides a related site, *www.accountingand-accountanting-tips.com,* which offers content, a message board, and a free newsletter.

Antiques and Collectables

If digging through garage sales, attending estate sales and scanning your local newspaper classifieds to find truly outstanding antique bargains is your thing, consider becoming an antique sales person. It's the perfect home business for people who know antique bargains when they find them. Resell these items for a profit by placing ads in antique-related magazines and newspapers, featuring them on your website, listing them on other websites and consigning your best items to well-attended antique auctions. The investment to start is minimal and so is the operating overhead. You'll need a van or a truck for transporting your inventory. Use the information and ideas in the following sections to create a business plan for antiques and collectables.

Business Overview

The Internet has become a boon to the antique sales business. This is true especially for selling smaller items that represent well in a photograph. Web sites for antique collectors number in the hundreds, but *eBay.com* has emerged as the most popular website. Selling via the Web has become so popular it has prompted some antique dealers to close their stores and move all their business to the Internet.

You need to do your homework in this business not only to price what you sell, but also because consumers are savvy and are discouraged from buying even very good items if the dealer is not knowledgeable. You will need to know about quality, materials, and origins before buying something that you want to resell. If the quality is good and the price is right, you will make money.

Antiques and Collectables Overview			
	Low	**Medium**	**High**
Cost to Start		*	
Operating Costs		*	
Potential Earnings		*	
Computer Skills		*	
Deadline Pressure	*		
Flexible Schedule		*	
Job Stress		*	

Marketing Antiques and Collectables

Many people prefer to buy antiques over the Internet. Collectibles sold on the Internet are typically below dealer prices. The Web opens the door to a world of customers a local seller would never see, many items are sold at higher prices than they could get locally. Some of the things to serve her customers well include setting up private pages where they can preview merchandise before it's publicly offered, sending out timely newsletters and guaranteeing satisfaction.

The more information you provide about what you're selling, the more apt you are to get favorable prices selling on the Web. When you demonstrate knowledge of what you are selling, people feel greater assurance they'll get what they hope they are paying for. The following list will give you some ideas on how to develop a marketing and sales base for an antiques and collectables business:

- Check collectors' club newsletters and Web sites that list items members want.

- Sell both low-end and high-end antiques at antique shows and flea markets.

- Sell on your own Web site and *eBay*. You will want to develop repeat customers. The Web also offers an ability to obtain inventory. Because it's difficult for buyers to distinguish quality, sellers often have to accept lower prices for their higher-quality items.

- Network with interior designers and decorators who can use you as a source.

- Look for inventory in places where there are large numbers of retirees, such as in Florida and Arizona. Be willing to bargain hard with thrift stores.

What to Charge

What you charge is the art and the science of this business. You can see what comparable services or products are selling for by following the bidding on websites like eBay and at big auction houses like Sotheby's and Christie's, which are available from their websites.

Financial Projections

Apply the information in the following financial projection table will help you setup your own financial projections in the templates covered in the Appendix.

Antiques and Collectables Business Financial Projections	
Funding Requirements	Projecting what you will expend starting up this business, which could be significant if you plan to acquire an inventory of antiques and collectables.
Income and Expenses	Projected total monthly revenue is subtracted from total monthly expenses to determine how much you plan to make each month.
Cash Flow	The cash flow projection is important because it can tell you the times during the year when you can expect a cash surplus

	and the times in the year when you can expect a cash shortage when you acquire inventory.
Assets and Liabilities	Includes all cash on hand and in bank accounts plus short-term investment that can be converted into cash in less than 30 days, such as certificates of deposits as assets.

Putting It All Together

The information sources in the table below will help you develop and finalize your business plan for an antique & collectable sales business. Sources for additional information are summarized as follows:

Associations

Contact the Antiques and Collectibles National Association (antiqueandcollectible.com) to learn more about the antique resale business.

Books & Publications

Antiques on the Cheap by James W. McKenzie and Jim McKenzie (Storey Books & Publications, 1998).

Antiques Roadshow Collectibles by Carol Prisant (Workman, 2003)

How to Start a Home-Based Antiques Business, Jacquelyn Peake (Globe Pequot Press, 2000)

Websites

www.collect.com-Antique Trader Weekly's Web site.
www.goantiques.com-on-line mall with a relationship to eBay that enables uploading items from your inventory to eBay.

TIAS *(www.TIAS.com)* member sites include *www.antiquearts.com,* an on-line mall, and w*ww.curioscape.com* with links to thousands of antique sites; *wuno.hovels.com,* which offers a free pricing guide; and *www.asheford.com* that offers a home-study course.

Cleaning Services

Cleaning services rank as the most common home business startups because it's relatively inexpensive to start up, easy to operate, and generate excellent revenues. You can operate a residential cleaning service focused on homes and apartments, stores and office buildings, or specialized in areas like carpet cleaning or ceiling cleaning. Promoting a cleaning business requires the use of fliers and coupons to get the word out. Contact the Cleaning and Maintenance Management Magazine Online (cmmonline.com) to learn more about the cleaning industry. Use the information and ideas in the following sections to create a business plan for cleaning services.

Business Overview

Providing cleaning services of all kinds is one of the fastest growing segments of the economy. The number of residential and commercial cleaning services more than doubled over the past five years. Of course, homes are not the only thing that needs cleaning. Every office and retail store and other commercial outlets use cleaning services. Usually people that startup a cleaning service chooses between home and commercial cleaning.

Cleaning Services Overview			
	Low	**Medium**	**High**
Cost to Start	*		
Operating Costs	*		
Potential Earnings		*	
Computer Skills	*		
Deadline Pressure		*	
Flexible Schedule		*	
Job Stress	*		

Marketing Cleaning Services

The key benefit you offer clients is providing them with a service that they do not have the time to do. The following list will give you some ideas on how to develop a marketing and sales base for a cleaning services business:

- Directly soliciting new home owners that are moving into your market area.

- Have your own Web page with its own domain name with testimonial letters from your clients. Have a website that identifies what services you offer so that potential customers using a search engine will find your site.

- List in the Yellow Pages is helpful for reaching business account customers

- Network face-to-face inside business and trade organizations such as the chamber of commerce and business referral organizations for business accounts

- Obtain referrals and doing overload with hotels and motels in your market area

- Call on retail stores and service firms within your market area and introduce yourself and your business.

What to Charge

How much should you charge will depend on the geographical area covered by your business? Most independent cleaning services charge by the hour with fees ranging between $25 and $75 an hour. Some charge below $25, and a few can command more than $75 an hour depending on locale and the industries they work in.

Financial Projections

Apply the information in the following financial projection table will help you setup your own financial projections in the templates covered in the Appendix.

Cleaning Services Business Financial Projections	
Funding Requirements	How much money is needed to acquire the supplies and equipment you'll need to start this business?
Income and Expenses	Projected total monthly revenue is subtracted from total monthly expenses to determine if you broke even or made money.
Cash Flow	Source of cash usually comes from service sales or the use of cash to pay for supplies and remaining cash after all expenses have been paid.
Assets and Liabilities	Assets are items that your business owns that have value, liabilities are debts that your business owes. The purpose of the balance sheet is to paint a picture of what your business is worth.

Putting It All Together

The information sources in the table below will help you develop and finalize your business plan for a cleaning services business. Sources for additional information are summarized as follows:

Associations

Building Service Contractors Association International; www.bscai.org (800) 368-3414

The International Window Cleaning Association; www.iwca.org
(703) 971-7771

Books & Publications

Cleaning Time Magazine; www.adpub.com/ctimes (800) 443-3433

Start Your Own Cleaning Service by Jacquelyn Lynn (Entrepreneur
Media, 2003)

How to Start a Home-Based Housecleaning Business by Melinda
Morse (Globe Pequot Press, 2002)

Websites

Cleaning Management Institute is a source of training and
education; wwwcminstitute.net
Contact Cleaning Consultants, Inc. publishes books, videos, and
software on cleaning services; www.cleaningconsultants.com (206)
682-9748

Computer Consulting

Would you like to turn the years of experience and the know-how you've accrued in your career mastering computer technology into an income? Computer consulting can become an ideal home-based business. Most offices have computers and a passing knowledge of how to use them. Your task will be to identify a niche in which you can market your expertise to business clients. Use the information and ideas in the following sections to create a computer consulting business plan.

Business Overview

Becoming known for your specialty in computers can be done by writing articles for publications apt to be read by prospective clients or appearing as the speaker at business organization meetings in your community. Personal networking trade associations and software user group meetings also help. The demand for computer consultants will remain strong in both small and large companies. To be a computer consultant, you must be technically proficient in one or more computer service areas (i.e., hardware and/or software). Pick a specialty in which your clients need lots of support. Effective consultants need to understand what clients want to accomplish and be able to offer what they want and need.

Computer Consulting Overview			
	Low	Medium	High
Cost to Start		*	
Operating Costs			*
Potential Earnings			*
Computer Skills			*
Deadline Pressure		*	
Flexible Schedule		*	
Job Stress			*

Marketing Computer Consulting

Your marketing task will be to identify your area of expertise and then sell yourself to particular clientele. If you're interested in developing custom software, then there are three primary software markets for you to consider: (1) corporate application software development, (2) retail software installation and (3) operational systems software support. Maybe you've been the "expert" at work who everyone turned to for computer advice and support. Now, you would like to get paid for doing what you've been doing in your career. You might specialize in working with small businesses that rely on readily available products like Windows and Office. When they change operating systems or equipment, they can run into compatibility problems they can't handle. So they will gladly pay a consultant who's willing to come to their office and make their systems work.

Call on companies that have an IT (information technology) staff and convey that you can relieve pressure on their staff. Have a website and use it effectively because clients look on the Web to find a specialist they need or for articles in computer publications. The following list will give you some ideas on how to develop a marketing and sales base for a computer consulting business:

- Networking face-to-face at business and trade association meetings for referrals and clients.

- Obtaining referrals from CPA and accounting firms and financial planners.

- Get listed as a support service professional in referral services that professional associations maintain for their members.

- Have a website that identifies what services you offer so that potential customers using a search engine can find your site.

- List your business in the Yellow Pages and your website in Web directories like switchboard.com and anywho.com. Getting listed on sites that relate to your specialty.

What to Charge

The median hourly rate for computer consultants is $75 an hour. Factors that influence rates include your specialization, what industry you work in, community size and location, the size and kind of clients you serve, the length of the project, and whether you work through a broker who finds work for you in return for 15 to 25 percent of your hourly rate. Bidding a fixed price for a job is risky until you have experience in pricing. Too high a bid is apt to scare off work, but too low a bid can cause heavy losses and lead to resenting your client, not the best attitude for developing a source of return and referral business.

Financial Projections

Apply the information in the following financial projection table will help you setup your own financial projections in the templates covered in the Appendix.

Computer Consulting Business Financial Projections	
Funding Requirements	Projecting what you will expend starting up this business should be minimal if you already have the computer equipment and software you need. If not, include those costs in your funding requirements worksheet.
Income and Expenses	Projected total monthly revenue is subtracted from total monthly expenses to determine how much you plan to make on a per hour basis.
Cash Flow	The cash flow projection shows how money will flow into the business in the form of cash and flow out of the business

	for paid expenses monthly.
Assets and Liabilities	The balance sheet lists your assets and liabilities, allowing you to determine what your net worth or equity position is in the business. Assets are items that your business owns that have a cash value. Liabilities are debts that your business owes. Your net worth is the difference between the two.

Putting It All Together

The information sources in the table below will help you develop and finalize your business plan for a computer consulting business. Sources for additional information are summarized as follows:

Associations

Institute for Certification of Computer Professionals: (847) 299-4227, (800) 843-8227 *www.iccp.org.*

Independent Computer Consultant's Association (ICCA): (800)*774-4222; www.icca.org.*

Books & Publications

The Computer Consultant's Workbook by Janet Ruhl (Technion Books & Publications, 1996)

Getting Started in Computer Consulting by Peter Meyer (John Wiley & Sons, 1999)

MCSE Consulting Bible by Harry M. Brelsford (John Wiley & Sons, 2001)

Websites

Janet Ruhl's Computer Consultant's Resource Page, *www.realrates.com*, with tips, results of compensation surveys, and more.

All about government contracting for computer consultants: *www.GovCon.com*

Computer Repair

If you've been the office guru everyone turned to when they encounter a problem with their personal computer, consider becoming a computer support specialist. You can get paid for doing what you've been doing for the company you use to work for. Offering computer support to individuals and small businesses can be an ideal home-based business. Most homes and offices have computers and a limited knowledge of how to use them, Use the information and ideas in the following sections to create your business plan.

A computer repair specialists must be technically proficient at resolving personal computer hardware and software problems because many time, a client requesting your services can not tell you if they're encountering a hardware or software problem. They just want the problem fixed. Computer specialists are also good at tutoring their clients on how to use their personal computers. In many cases, the problem they were hired to resolve was caused by a lack of knowledge on behalf of their client. Use the information and ideas in the following sections to create a computer repairs business plan.

Business Overview

The demand for computer repair specialists will remain strong, particularly among firms with fewer than ten employees or are an active home-based computer user. Effective specialist need to understand what clients want to accomplish, why they're having problems, and what they can do to resolve the problem. They need to describe what they propose to do in a way that makes sense from the client's perspective.

Computer Repairs Overview			
	Low	**Medium**	**High**
Cost to Start		*	
Operating Costs		*	
Potential Earnings			*
Computer Skills			*
Deadline Pressure			*
Flexible Schedule		*	
Job Stress		*	

Marketing Computer Repairs

Everybody has a computer and at some point, many will need a computer specialist to assist them in solving a hardware or software problem. So, why would anybody be interested in paying you for your computer support? If you are willing to visit your clients in their offices or homes to offer them personal computer support, then this market is wide open. The key benefit you offer clients is confidence that you can solve their problems without over charging them.

You might specialize in working with small businesses that rely on readily available products like Windows and Office, but when they change operating systems or equipment they run into compatibility problems they can't handle. They can't afford to spend hours of time wading through help lines, but most consultants serving this market only have superficial knowledge of installing new versions of Windows. So they will gladly pay a consultant who will come to their office and make their systems work with a minimum of time and stress. The key benefits you offer clients are providing a higher skill level than they can afford to get by hiring a full-time employee. The following list will give you some ideas on how to develop a marketing and sales base for a computer repair business:

- Mount a magnetic sign or decal on your vehicle featuring your service and displaying your phone number and website.

- Network face-to-face inside business and trade organizations meetings.

- Obtain referrals financial planners and personal tax accounts.

- Get listed as a support service that professional associations maintain for their members.

- Have a website that identifies what services you offer so that potential customers using a search engine will find your site.

- Call on retail stores and service firms that deal with computers in your market area and introduce your business.

- List your business in the Yellow Pages and your website in Web directories like switchboard.com and anywho.com.

What to Charge

The median hourly rate for computer repair people is $50 an hour, but some get $25 an hour while still others charge $100 an hour or more. Factors that influence rates include your specialization, community size and location, the size and kind of clients you serve.

Financial Projections

Apply the information in the following financial projection table will help you setup your own financial projections in the templates covered in the Appendix.

Computer Repairs Business Financial Projections	
Funding Requirements	Projecting what you will expend starting up your business is a critical component of the startup process.
Income and Expenses	Projected total monthly revenue is subtracted from total monthly expenses to determine it you broke even or made money to make on a per hour basis.
Cash Flow	For new start-ups, the cash flow projections are important because it tells you the times in the year when you can expect a cash surplus and the times when you can expect a cash shortage.
Assets and Liabilities	The balance sheet lists your assets and liabilities, allowing you to determine what your net worth or equity position is in the business. Assets are items that your business owns that have a cash value. Liabilities are debts that your business owes. Your net worth is the difference between the two.

Putting It All Together

The information sources in the table below will help you develop and finalize your business plan for a computer repair business. Sources for additional information are summarized as follows:

Associations

Independent Computer Consultant's Association (ICCA): (800)*774-4222; www.icca.org.*

Books & Publications

The Computer Consultant's Workbook by Janet Ruhl (Technion Books & Publications, 1996)

Getting Started in Computer Consulting by Peter Meyer (John Wiley & Sons, 1999)

MCSE Consulting Bible by Harry M. Brelsford (John Wiley & Sons, 2001)

Websites

Janet Ruhl's Computer Consultant's Resource Page, *www.realrates.com,* with tips, results of compensation surveys, and more.

All about government contracting for computer consultants: *www.GovCon.com*

To learn more about this business, contact the National Association of Computer Repair (www.nacrbo.com).

Contractor Services

If you have carpentry or another construction skill, you can run a profitable contractor business from your home. Numerous homeowners remodel or add to their homes each year. A contractor's license and the appropriate tools and skills to handle a variety of jobs let you provide valuable services to homeowners and business contractors. You can advertise at home shows and through all the traditional means, including a website and build relationships with other contractors in areas where they can use your assistance for larger jobs. Before starting out, you should check the going rate for contractors in your market and charge accordingly. Contact the Associated Builders and Contractors (www.abc.org) for more information.

Business Overview

At some point in time, every house or commercial building will need to be remodeled or undergo some repairs. This is where the independent contractor comes in. Remodeling a room for homes and commercial buildings can become a great startup business that will keep you as busy as you want to be. It requires some skill and know-how with tools, so if you have a background in contracting and enjoy a variety of jobs, offering contract services could be an enjoyable full-time or part-time business for you. Use the information and ideas in the following sections to create a contractor services business plan.

Contractor Services Overview			
	Low	Medium	High
Cost to Start		*	
Operating Costs		*	
Potential Earnings		*	
Computer Skills	*		
Deadline Pressure		*	
Flexible Schedule	*		
Job Stress		*	

Marketing Contractor Services

The key benefits you offer clients are availability and being less expensive than trade personnel.

Trust is fundamental to this business. Customers need to be able to leave you a list and the key and know the job will be done and their house will be standing when they get back. As a contractor, you may find yourself doing almost anything you're willing to do, including hanging wallpaper, painting, installing flooring, electrical wiring, and replacing tiles. You need to have all the tools required to do whatever services you provide.

Referrals are the number-one way to build a clientele. Give yourself time to develop a sufficient number of customers so that you're turning down work instead of looking for it. Dressing presentably and neatly separates you from the workers people are suspicious of when they see them in their neighborhoods. The following list will give you some ideas on how to develop a marketing and sales base for a contractor services business:

- Make yourself indispensable to someone with a fixer-upper is one way to stay busy for several months or even years. Let people know what you are doing in your personal circles.

- Solicit businesses in condominium complexes as often the owners don't have tools and equipment to do home improvement and repairs.

- Call on business offices and leaving fliers.

- Have attractive signage on your truck or vehicle with your phone number and website visible.

- If you live in or near a resort area where people have second homes, soliciting absent owners for off-season work.

- Network inside business and trade organizations such as the chamber of commerce.

- Create a website that identifies what services you offer so that potential customers using a search engine will find your site.

- Call on hardware and home furnishing stores in your market area and introduce yourself and your business.

- List your business in the Yellow Pages and your website in directories like *switchboard.com* and *anywho.com*.

What to Charge

A rule of thumb is to charge half the rates plumbers and electricians get, whose overhead costs are higher. There's a large variation from $15 an hour in low-cost areas to $80 an hour major in metropolitan areas. The rate for emergency or after-hours service may be up to double the regular hourly rate. Most independent contractors charge by the hour with fees ranging between $25 and $75 an hour and a few can command more than $75 an hour depending on locale and the industries they work in.

Financial Projections

Apply the information in the following financial projection table will help you setup your own financial projections in the templates covered in the Appendix.

Contractor Services Business Financial Projections	
Funding Requirements	Projecting what you will expend starting up your business is a critical component of a contractor services business if you will need to acquire substantial equipment and special clothing.

Income and Expenses	Projected total monthly revenue is subtracted from total monthly expenses to determine how much you plan to make on a per hour basis.
Cash Flow	Knowing what your cash position is enables you to manage your money and it gives you the opportunity to secure working capital funding to avoid running out of cash when you have projected a cash shortage.
Assets and Liabilities	The purpose of the balance sheet is to paint a picture of what your business is worth at any one moment in time. Not included on the balance sheet are non-tangible assets such as goodwill and contingent liabilities such as future warranty claims.

Putting It All Together

The information sources in the table below will help you develop and finalize your business plan for a contractor services business. Sources for additional information are summarized as follows:

Associations

Associated Builders and Contractors; www.abc.org (703) 812-2000

Books & Publications

Handyman's Handbook, David Koenigsberg (McGraw-Hill Professional, 2003)

Buy It, Fix It, and Sell It by Kevin C. Myers (Dearborn Trade Publishing, 1997)

Websites

House Doctors Handyman Service: (800) 319-3359, (513) 831-0100;   *www.housedoctors.com* Guide and CDs: *www.handyman-business.com*

Natural Handyman: *www.naturalhandyman.com*

Desktop Publishing

Desktop publishing is one of the fastest growing professions in the computer services industry. Their numbers have doubled over the last 5 years to in excess of 100,000. Although most are not self-employed, solo desktop publishers are growing in number as more companies are outsourcing their publishing tasks. To become successful as an independent desktop publisher, you will need to focus your message on what you do well (i.e., the written word, graphics, creative design, etc.). Use the information and ideas in the following sections to create a desktop publishing business plan.

Business Overview

If you have an eye for creativity and problem solving, like to write with proficiency for using illustrations and graphics to supplement your written material, and then you may have the essential ingredients for starting up a desktop publishing business. Use the information and ideas in the following sections to create your business plan.

Courses on how to use desktop publishing software and related graphic, photo-editing, and Web-page design programs are available at community colleges and trade schools. Many of these programs issue certificates. Courses in how to use desktop software programs are available from the companies that make these products. Contact Adobe (www.adobe.com/misc/training.html) or QuarkXPress (www.quark.com).

Desktop Publishing Overview		
	Low	Medium	High
Cost to Start		*	
Operating Costs	*		
Potential Earnings		*	
Computer Skills			*
Deadline Pressure			*
Flexible Schedule		*	
Job Stress		*	

Marketing Desktop Publishing

Desktop publishers turn clients' marketing intentions into multiple kinds of documents such as catalogues, brochures, manuals, directories, and Web postings. For each publication, desktop publishers create the words for the document and format the final document complete with illustrations to satisfy their clients' request. The key benefits you offer clients are providing a higher skill level than they can afford to get by hiring a full-time employee.

Freelance opportunities for desktop publishers and editorial services are expanding because of the increasing use of websites that constantly demand new content. Many publishing houses and news papers have reduced staff, so desktop publishing has become more of a freelance industry. Many desktop publishers offer editing services to their credentials. If you're breaking into desktop publishing, offering basic editing services is a good way to break into the more lucrative desktop publishing jobs.

Project editing is where you manage and coordinate the writing process for a book or other types of publication from beginning to end.

Developmental editing where you work with a client to develop or rework an initial concept into a well-organized publication.

Copy editing where you review a manuscript after it is considered complete. They check facts, make style improvement changes, check for consistency, and reword to correct grammar or improve clarity.

Proofreading where you read a manuscript word for word when it is in galley form (i.e., on the printing press ready to go). It is the last check made that a manuscript is free of spelling and grammar errors before it's printed.

The following list will give you some ideas on how to develop a marketing and sales base for a desktop publishing business:

- Contact all of the publishing firms in your state and if they use freelancers, find out what you need to do to get on their list.

- Many publishing firms are willing to hire freelancers from anywhere in the country because it is a service that can be performed with without requiring face-to-face contact. Writers Market is a book that's available at the research desk of most libraries. It lists contact information for most of the publishers in the country

- Bid on work for firms that post their projects for freelancers on their websites, such as elance.com, guru.com and freelanceonline.com.

- Get on the bidding list for local, state, and federal government work. School districts also use desktop publishing services.

- Local small-business clients may require more of your time to determine what their needs are, but they can become regular clients.

- Promote your services in a well designed flyer and website that addresses your editorial, graphic, and creative layout skills

What to Charge

Most desktop publishers charge by the hour with fees ranging between $25 and $75 an hour depending on locale and the industries they work in.

Financial Projections

Apply the information in the following financial projection table will help you setup your own financial projections in the templates covered in the Appendix.

Desktop Publishing Business Financial Projections	
Funding Requirements	Projecting what you will expend starting up this business should be minimal if you already have the computer equipment and software you need. If not, include those costs in your funding requirements worksheet.
Income and Expenses	Projected total monthly revenue is subtracted from total monthly expenses to determine how much you plan to make.
Cash Flow	Source of cash usually come from service sales. Your use of cash to meet expenses is deducted to determine remaining cash, which is the total source of cash for each month.

Assets and Liabilities	The purpose of the balance sheet is to paint a picture of what your business is worth at any one moment in time. Not included on the balance sheet are non-tangible assets such as goodwill and contingent liabilities such as future warranty claims.

Putting It All Together

The information sources in the table below will help you develop and finalize your business plan for a desktop publishing business. Sources for additional information are summarized as follows:

Associations

desktoppublishing.com is one of the most comprehensive sites covering a variety of desktop publishing subjects. The site features several free desktop publishing tools you can use to create a document.

Books & Publications

Start and Run a Desktop Publishing Business by Barbara Fanson (Self Counsel Press 2004)

Websites

Jumpola.com is an excellent site list several sources you can visit to learn more about what it takes to become a successful desktop publisher. Free photos are featured that can be used in your desktop publishing documents. Supplier sources are also identified.
Elance.com is a site to advertise (free) your availability to make your desktop publishing services available and it lists jobs that are available for desktop publishers.

Courses in how to use desktop software programs are available from the companies that make these products. Contact Adobe

(www.adobe.com/misc/training.html) or QuarkXPress
(www.quark.com).

Direct Sales

Companies that hire home-based direct sellers call their salespeople by different names such as distributors, representatives, or sales consultants. Whatever name they use, they're all independent salespeople. Just about everything is being sold these days are through direct sales, including books, videos, CDs, computers, children's toys, artwork, kitchenware, cookware and cutlery, cleaning products, decorating items, small appliances like vacuum cleaners, men's clothing, luxury women's clothing, baby products, jewelry, health equipment, candles, air filters, water-treatment systems, Internet and telecommunications services, rubber stamps, plants, gift baskets, gift items, encyclopedias, and more. The diversity of direct sales products and services is endless. Some couples go into the direct-sales business together focusing on what each does best-one sells the products and maintains contacts while the other develops sales prospects. Use the information and ideas in the following sections to create a direct sales business plan.

Business Overview

If you have an outgoing personality and love selling the products you represent, you can make money and enjoy direct selling. Use the online National Association of Manufacturers (nam.org) website to find companies that are interested in hiring manufacturer's representative that work out of their home. Once you have identified the right products and conducted a market analysis into their viability in your area, use the directory to contact the manufacturers of the products you're interested in selling.

Direct Sales Overview			
	Low	Medium	High
Cost to Start	*		
Operating Costs		*	
Potential Earnings			*
Computer Skills	*		
Deadline Pressure	*		
Flexible Schedule			*
Job Stress			*

Marketing Direct Sales

Working as a manufacturer's representative means you promote and market the products on a city, state or even a national basis. You sell the manufacturer's products to target customers, be it businesses or consumers. Always try to negotiate exclusive service contracts with the manufacturers so you represent them within geographic boundaries specified in an agreement. Also, you'll want to have a good working knowledge in the type of products you'll be selling.

People who sign up with direct-selling companies do so to earn extra income, because they believe in the product, and to obtain items they use at discounted prices. For actually selling products, a passion for the product is more important than anything else. If you're naturally upbeat and treat people well regardless of how you feel, you're a candidate for direct selling. The following list will give you some ideas on how to develop a marketing and sales base for a direct sales business:

- Attending events where you can meet people, such as craft fairs, Bible-study classes, senior-citizen centers, and mobile-home parks. Some direct sellers make contacts standing in lines and at bus stops. Because direct selling is face-to-face, be well-groomed and personable.

- Have a website that identifies what products and services you offer so that potential customers using a search engine will find your site. While only a small percentage of direct selling is done over the Internet, some people do manage to use their websites to make sales.

- Keeping in regular contact with your customers and down-lining via the phone, e-mail, postcards, and meetings. Incentivizing your down-line with regular financial, travel, and other rewards that recognize achievement.

What to Charge

Remuneration can be by way of a commission charged on sales or you can mark up your wholesale costs on the goods you control to set a price. Prices of the products and services you sell for a direct selling company is determined by them. What you earn is based on the commission structure of what you are selling so be sure you fully understand the commission structure.

Financial Projections

Apply the information in the following financial projection table will help you setup your own financial projections in the templates covered in the Appendix.

	Direct Sales Business Financial Projections
Funding Requirements	Projecting what you will expend starting up this business should be minimal if you already have the computer equipment you need. If not, include those costs in your funding requirements worksheet.
Income and Expenses	Projected total monthly revenue is subtracted from total monthly expenses to determine it you broke even or made money to make on a per hour basis.
Cash Flow	Use of cash is money paid out to cover the expenses of the business that are due in a particular month.

Assets and Liabilities	Includes all cash on hand and in bank accounts plus short-term investment that can be converted into cash in less than 30 days, such as certificates of deposits as assets.

Putting It All Together

The information sources in the table below will help you develop and finalize your business plan for a direct selling business. Sources for additional information are summarized as follows:

Associations

The Direct Selling Association (DSA); dsa.org (202) 452-8866

Books & Publications

Network Marketing in the 21st Century, Richard Poe (Prima Lifestyles, 1999)

Your First Year in Network Marketing by Mark and Rene Reid Yarnell (Prima Lifestyles, 1998)

Websites

Comcast offers direct sales positions throughout the country at www.comcastdsrjobs.com

Secrets of Building a Million Dollar Network Marketing Organization From a Guy Who's Been There Done That and Shows You How to Do It To by Joe Rubino (Upline Press, 2000)

Energy Management Consulting

Corporations spend billions of dollars annually on energy to light, heat and air condition their buildings. With soaring energy costs, taking care of the environment and saving money have become concerns for everyone. The future for energy management consulting looks very bright, but you will need to take the time and effort to become an expert in the field. If you have enterprise this area that perhaps you can supplement it with training, depending on your background, you can become an energy management consultant.

You'll teach business managers practical and useful energy management techniques for reducing their energy consumption. Contact the United States Department of Energy (energy.gov) and *The* Energy Management Institute (energyinstitution.org) to learn more about energy management. Use the information and ideas in the following sections to create an energy management consulting business plan.

Business Overview

The demand for energy management consultants will remain strong, particularly among manufacturing firms. You'll need to decide upon the scope of your services you want to specialize in. Some consultants offer complete services while others stick to electric service use. Often you can draw on your experience in energy management. Having had a career in energy management, for example, might help in developing a specialty in investigating energy use; a background in an art field could be useful working with local, state and federal government agencies. First-rate computer skills are vital, as are creativity and intuition when it comes to knowing how to develop leads energy management clients.

Energy Management Consulting Overview			
	Low	Medium	High
Cost to Start		*	
Operating Costs		*	
Potential Earnings			*
Computer Skills		*	
Deadline Pressure		*	
Flexible Schedule		*	
Job Stress	*		

Marketing Energy Management Consulting

The key benefits you offer clients are providing a higher skill level than they can afford to get by hiring a full-time employee. The following list will give you some ideas on how to develop a marketing and sales base for an energy management consulting business:

- Directly soliciting high energy use companies like manufacturing firms.

- Give seminar presentations and speeches

- Have a booth at conventions of high energy use industries

- Have your own Web page with its own domain name with testimonial letters and any articles you have written. Have a website that identifies what services you offer so that potential customers using a search engine will find your site.

- Listing in the Yellow Pages is helpful for reaching the general public about energy consulting work for corporations

- Participate in trade associations and professional organizations for the type of clientele you are seeking
.

- Show your expertise by writing articles and letters to the editors of newspapers and business journals. This can lead to being used as a source by journalists.

- Network face-to-face inside business and trade organizations such as the chamber of commerce and business referral organizations.

- Get listed as a support service in referral services that professional associations maintain for their members.

What to Charge

How much should you charge will depend on the geographical area covered by your business? Most independent accountants charge by the hour with fees ranging between $75 and $175 an hour. Some charge below $75 an hour depending on locale and the industries they work in.

Financial Projections

Apply the information in the following financial projection table will help you setup your own financial projections in the templates covered in the Appendix.

Energy Management Business Consulting Financial Projections	
Funding Requirements	Projecting what you will expend starting up this business should be a minimal component of the startup process.
Income and Expenses	Projected total monthly revenue is subtracted from total monthly expenses to determine it you broke even or made

	money to make on a per hour basis.
Cash Flow	Cash balance is the more important of the two since it shows your projected cash balance for each month and it should always be above zero.
Assets and Liabilities	Includes all cash on hand and in bank accounts plus short-term investment that can be converted into cash in less than 30 days and all investments, such as certificate of deposits as assets.

Putting It All Together

The information sources in the table below will help you develop and finalize your business plan for an energy management consulting business. Sources for additional information are summarized as follows:

Associations

Association of Energy Service Professionals; www.aesp.org (480) 704-5900

Books & Publications

Energy Management Handbook by Wayne Turner (2009)

Websites

Energy Watchdog features the latest in energy conservation; www.energywatchdog.com (814) 861-3655

Environmental Consulting

Environmental inspections are becoming a must for nearly all business real estate transactions and construction projects. Lenders require them because of concern about potential liability and the growing number of people who are becoming concerned about the environment. Lenders require them because of the concern about potential liability created by the Comprehensive Environmental Response, Compensation and Liability Act (CERCLA), known as the Superfund. This act mandates inspection and remediation of environmental hazards. Also as growing numbers of people are becoming more aware and concerned about environmental hazards, they too want the information environmental inspections provide. If environmental issues are one of your areas of expertise, then there are a number of opportunities for you to consider in this field. Use the information and ideas in the following sections to create an environmental consulting business plan.

Business Overview

There are three types or "phases" of environmental assessment – Phase 1, 2 and 3. Phases 1 and 2 can be the basis of starting up a home business.

Phase 1 is a review phase done by someone who has been trained to use the specific steps prescribed by the American Society of Testing Materials for identifying whether hazardous substances and petroleum products may be present in the structure or in the groundwater, or surface water of a property.

Phase 2 involves taking samples of possibly contaminated materials, surfaces, or subsurface materials and testing them, sometimes in a laboratory. The scope of tests may include soil testing, measuring the quantity and quality of well water, searching for volatile organic compounds around an oil tank, checking roofing and tiling materials for asbestos, confirming that painted surfaces do not contain lead, testing indoor air quality and sampling the air from air conditioning ducts, looking beneath the house and carpeting for live and dead mold, and many other tests.

Phase 3 consists of remedial activities to clean up the problems such as removing asbestos and PCBs, removing lead paint, cleaning up contaminated soil, and removing and disposing of hazardous waste. The contractors who do things of this nature are usually not home-based businesses.

In order do Phase 1 and Phase 2 assessments as a business, you need to obtain the required training, certification, and licensing. Since these requirements vary by state, check with your state about training you need to do environmental assessments. You can check the licensing for your state on the Internet through links provided by the Council on Licensure, Enforcement and Regulation (CLEAR) at *www.clearhq.orgl boards.htm.*

Environmental Consulting Overview			
	Low	**Medium**	**High**
Cost to Start		*	
Operating Costs		*	
Potential Earnings			*
Computer Skills		*	
Deadline Pressure		*	
Flexible Schedule		*	
Job Stress	*		

Marketing Environmental Consulting

Inspections can indicate conditions such as contaminated soil, vegetation damage, or the presence of molds, mildew, allergens, lead paint, asbestos, radon, electromagnetic radiation, water leaks, or just old storage tanks lying beneath the surface. In order to avoid liability under CERCLA, a new property owner needs a report to establish that he or she has no reason to believe any hazardous substance has been discharged on the property. Credentials matter, so the time and money you invest in getting them help both with credibility and your professional standing compared with those who don't have them.

Referrals from professionals and companies involved in real estate transactions will be responsible for most of the work you get. Occasionally, owners of property will order an inspection unrelated to the property being involved in a current real estate transaction. Develop a relationship with attorneys, mortgage companies, banks and other lenders. Consider beginning your business in an area where there is a lot of new construction going on or where there has been a known history of contaminants that might cause many home sellers and buyers to insist on having environmental assessments whenever property changes hands.

What to Charge

How much should you charge will depend on the geographical area covered by your business? Most independent accountants charge by the hour with fees ranging between $50 and $150 an hour. Some charge below $50 an hour depending on locale and the industries they work in.

Financial Projections

Apply the information in the following financial projection table will help you setup your own financial projections in the templates covered in the Appendix.

Environmental Consulting Business Financial Projections	
Funding Requirements	Projecting what you will expend starting up your business is a critical component of the startup process.
Income and Expenses	Projected total monthly revenue is subtracted from total monthly expenses to determine how much you plan to make on a per hour basis.

Cash Flow	The cash flow projection shows how money will flow into your business in the form of revenues and flow out of the business in the form of expenses.
Assets and Liabilities	The total value of physical assets owned by the business including equipment and furnishings are listed in the asset column of the balance sheet. The total sum of money owed to your product and service suppliers for outstanding invoices, including items such as inventory and utility bills are recorded under liabilities.

Putting It All Together

The information sources in the table below will help you develop and finalize your business plan for an environmental consulting business. Sources for additional information are summarized as follows:

Associations

Environmental Assessment Association (EAA) offers five degree designations. (320) 763-4320; *www.iami.org*

Books & Publications

Environmental Assessment in Practice, D. Owen Harrop and Ashley Nixon (Routledge, 1999)

Environmental Site Assessment, Phase I, Kathleen Hess and Kathleen Hess-Kosa (Lewis Publishers, 1997)

Websites

ICF International is a global environmental service firm; www.ifci.com

Estate Sales

Tens of millions of homes are overstuffed with possessions that the owner would like to get rid of and make some money in the process. While the term estate sale implies a death, other occasions prompt sales needing the services of a professional, such as moving and divorce.

When disposing of household contents, most people want to make some money in the process, and estate sales managers enable them to get more for their stuff than they could get on their own. Estate sales specialist enables them to get more for their stuff than they could get on their own. Besides increasing sales, estate sales specialists do the time consuming work of sorting, cleaning, repairing, organizing, arranging, showing, pricing, advertising, and selling, and haul off items.

The service may also involve disposing of unsold items in a number of possible ways, such as donating them to charity, selling them to a dealer or on *eBay,* or returning them to the owner. So clearly a professional estate sales specialist takes the stress out of disposing of items before a major move or after a death in the family. Use the information and ideas in the following sections to create a business plan for estate sales.

Business Overview

The key benefits you offer clients are a higher return on their goods, relief from stress, time savings, and convenience. Estate sales involve handling a lot of specialized details and can be overwhelming to anyone without the prope~erleilce or organizing skill. An individual may miss things of value or incorrectly price costly items. Specialization possibilities include handling particular kinds of goods, like furniture, or dealing with particular situations, like downsizing. Being able to take credit cards and do instant check verification will increase sales. No-return policies are standard in this business.

No special training or certification is required to manage an estate sale. It is important, though, to have knowledge of the items you are dealing with. Some may be extremely valuable and others may not have much value. If you understand the worth of the commodities you are handling, you will have a better idea of where and to whom to sell them to make the most money for your client and yourself. Since an estate-sale agent links buyers to sellers, it is important to keep abreast of who is buying what and where. For example, a particular make of china may sell better through a collector's club or listing than it will on *eBay*. Your research and experience will help you figure out the best places to list the items you handle.

Estate Sales Overview			
	Low	**Medium**	**High**
Cost to Start		*	
Operating Costs		*	
Potential Earnings		*	
Computer Skills		*	
Deadline Pressure		*	
Flexible Schedule		*	
Job Stress		*	

Marketing Estate Sales

In building this business, you need to develop a customer base of collectors. You can do this by subscribing to collector associations and societies, which charge an annual fee, and developing your own collector database as you go. First conduct a free, no-obligation interview and inspection with the responsible party. Provide honest feedback about your option for selling the items, as well as the likely costs and outcomes.

Once the client agrees to hire you to conduct the sale, the cleaning and sorting begins. If anything needs to be repaired, organized, or arranged, this is the time to do it. The groundwork is put in place for a successful estate sale at this time, and personal or keepsake items are set aside for the family.

Next, all the items are researched as to value and priced. Do this step with a family member present to prevent misunderstandings. The client gets a list of the inventory before and after the sale occurs. If you do not have experience with appraisal, you may want to take a course or hire someone to help with this as it is crucial to a successful sale.

Regardless of the preparation, the proceeds of a sale will not be what they could be if the sale is not advertised properly to people who are interested in what is being sold. Again, connecting the right buyers with the products they want is the real goal of this service. Estate sales can be advertised in local newspapers and trade magazines and are open to anyone who stops by. Sales also can be conducted on an "appointment only" basis-appropriate, for example, in gated communities. In this case, buyers can preview photos and descriptions of items at a "virtual estate sale" posted on a website or printed for distribution so only interested buyers actually come to the sale. The type of goods being sold to the buyer base and the location of the sale determine what will be the best type of sale to hold. When a sale is in progress, especially if it is held at the client's property, security is important. The following list will give you some ideas on how to develop a marketing and sales base for an estate sales business:

- Place ads in the newsletters of different .collector societies related to the kinds of items your client has to sell (e.g., the American Pottery Club).

- Developing referral relationships with family, friends and associates.

- Have a website with your services and contact information displayed. Use key words that identify your community and specialties so people using a search engine will find your site. Websites for collectors are good places to list your website and will help in generating traffic for your site.

- List your business in the Yellow Pages and your website in directories at *switchboard. com* and *anywho.com.*

- Advertise in publications such as auction house catalogues, real estate journals, and trust fund magazines

What to Charge

Usually a commission of 25 to 40 percent of total sales is charged for this service. Advertising costs are subtracted before calculating the commission. Payment is made after the sale is finished. The commission varies depending on the quality and quantity of the stock as well as the amount of work involved to coordinate the sale.

Financial Projections

Apply the information in the following financial projection table will help you setup your own financial projections in the templates covered in the Appendix.

Estate Sales Business Financial Projections	
Funding Requirements	Projecting what you will expend starting up your business is a critical component of the startup process.
Income and Expenses	Projected total monthly revenue is subtracted from total monthly expenses to determine if you broke even or made money.
Cash Flow	The cash flow projection is important because it can tell you the times during the year when you can expect a cash surplus and the times in the year when you can expect a cash shortage.
Assets and Liabilities	The total value of physical assets owned by the business including equipment and furnishings are listed in the asset column of the balance sheet. The total sum of money owed to your product and service suppliers for outstanding invoices, including items

	such as inventory and utility bills are recorded under liabilities.

Putting It All Together

The information sources in the table below will help you develop and finalize your business plan for an accounting service business. Sources for additional information are summarized as follows:

Associations

The Appraisers Association of America has a certification program. (212) 889-5404 *www.appraisersassoc.org*

American Society of Appraisers offers accreditation: (703) 478-2228 *www.appraisers.org*

New England Appraisers Association: (802) 228-7444 *www.newenglandappraisers.net*

Books & Publications

The Complete Guidebook to the Business of Tag and Estate Sales by Mim Nagy (TLC Tag Sales and Publishing Co., 2002)

Garage Sale & Flea Market Annual, Beth Summers and Karen Smith (Collector Books & Publications, 2003)

Websites

Garage Sale Zone offers free listings and free printable signs at *www.garagesalezone.com*
This Vancouver estate sale service sells an "Estate Sale Business Starter Kit" *www.estatesales.bc.ca*

Event Planning

If you have an attention to detail and organization, good communication skills, and a creative flair, which are all personal traits shared by event planners, then perhaps you should consider starting an event planning business. Event planners are responsible for organizing and hosting 'special events for their clients, with duties that can include creating and sending out invitations, selecting event locations, acquiring decorations, arranging entertainers and speakers, selecting caterers and creating menus, and just about everything else necessary for staging a special event. You can specialize in family events such as weddings, anniversaries, birthdays, graduations and award ceremonies or you can focus on corporate events, including luncheons, parties, grand openings, investor meetings and trade shows.

If you talk to families who are planning a major event like a wedding, you will hear a lot of reasons why they're willing to hire an event planner. Event planners can help them save money and get more from the money they spend. Here's how to get started as an event planner:

- If you talk to wedding planners, you'll hear a lot of reasons why more and more couples are choosing to hire them:

- In a down economy, we help people save money; in an up economy, we help them spend more opulently.

- Since more and more couples today both work, they are simply too busy to plan their own weddings and chances are the bride's mother is working, too.

- Couples want to distinguish themselves among their cohorts, and their wedding is their big chance to make a statement about how they can throw a party.

The average age of a bride has climbed from twenty in 1982 to twenty-seven in 2002, and the length of the average engagement is now sixteen months. This means couples have more time to save money and plan for the wedding of their dreams.

The fact is, all these reasons are valid and the conclusion is wedding planning can be a profitable business for someone with the right skills and talent. There's plenty of potential business-so far only 1 in 8 of the 2.5 million weddings in the United States hire a wedding consultant. So there's a huge untapped market. But what exactly do wedding planners do? The answer is nearly anything and everything the bride and groom want them to do. The range of services you can offer is endless. Use the information and ideas in the following sections to create a business plan for event planning.

Business Overview

To succeed in this business, you should be detail oriented yet creative so you can produce on-time perfect events with so much flair and style that the wedding seems as though it cost more than it did. You must be an expert in wedding etiquette, traditions, and scheduling, as well as diplomatic and good at calming nerves, soothing rumpled feathers, and keeping argumentative relatives from disrupting the joyous event. To learn more about the event planning business, contact Event Planner (www.event-planner. com).

Event Planning Overview			
	Low	**Medium**	**High**
Cost to Start	*		
Operating Costs		*	
Potential Earnings			*
Computer Skills		*	
Deadline Pressure			*
Flexible Schedule		*	
Job Stress			*

Marketing Event Planning

Be aware that the wedding and event planning field is increasingly competitive. A full-time wedding coordinator working alone can service forty weddings a year. You should expect June, August, September, and October to be your busiest months, with January your slowest. But be aware that your clients can save significant money by booking their wedding in a slow month. Wedding consulting is a glamour business, so you need to spend money on your own wardrobe, makeup, and hairstyling to project your own image to your clientele. You can branch out to plan other types of events such as corporate meetings and bar mitzvahs, particularly in smaller communities, where there may not be enough weddings for a full-time business. The following list will give you some ideas on how to develop a marketing and sales base for an event planning business:

- Calling on and networking with others providing wedding services: photographers, printers, florists, hotel and banquet-hall managers, bakeries, makeup artists, jewelers, caterers, travel agents, musicians, and disc jockeys. However, some wedding planners indicate that this does not work well for them.

- Joining and participating in professional, community, trade, and religious organizations in your community to make yourself known.

- List in the Yellow Pages, which will enable you to be found on Web directories like *switchboard.com* and *anywho.com*. Consider ads on local directory sites like *Yahoo Get Local* and *SuperPages*.

- Advertise in specialty wedding publications or guides and wedding supplements to local newspapers. Exhibiting at bridal shows is expensive but may produce business.

- Have a website linked to many wedding-related sites. The Web is especially important for wedding coordinators located in destination locations-vacation places where people like to get married.

- Use direct mail to recipients of wedding-planning guides and sending out newsletters to prospective and past clients.

- Offer free consultations for couples, advising them of what will be involved in planning their wedding. Use this time to establish a trusting relationship and to gather information for a written proposal you can submit to them after the meeting.

- Teaching adult education courses on how to plan a wedding.

- Get repeat business by doing parties and other events such as anniversaries for your clients, their family, and their friends.

- Get listed in directories like *Modernbride.com* and *weddingchannel.com*.

What to Charge

But, of course, you as your own boss can limit the number of weddings you take on to fit your financial and lifestyle preferences. If you choose you might do only do eight, not eighty, weddings a year. You can begin by organizing a wedding for a friend or relative for free to build your portfolio. Be sure to get pictures from the photographer and letters of recommendation from the bride.

Wedding coordinators may charge a flat fee, a per-diem rate, or an hourly rate for their services. Flat fees may be from 10 to 15 percent of the wedding budget, which is now estimated at $22,000 to $27,000. Per-diem rates range from $300 to $1,200. Hourly rates range from $50 to $150. As expected, location influences pricing. Wedding coordinators should not expect to derive commissions from referrals they make; this is frowned on professionally and discouraged legally. However, coordinators can increase their revenue by providing extra services such as renting tuxedos, printing invitations, and selling accessories like party gifts.

Financial Projections

Apply the information in the following financial projection table will help you setup your own financial projections in the templates covered in the Appendix.

Event Planning Business Financial Projections	
Funding Requirements	Projecting what you will expend starting up this business should be minimal if you already have the computer equipment you need. If not, include those costs in your funding requirements worksheet.
Income and Expenses	Projected total monthly revenue is subtracted from total monthly expenses to determine how much you plan to make on a per hour basis.
Cash Flow	The cash flow projection shows how money will flow into the business in the form of cash and flow out of the business for paid expenses monthly.
Assets and Liabilities	The total value of physical assets owned by the business including equipment and furnishings are listed in the asset column of the balance sheet. The total sum of money owed to your product and service suppliers for outstanding invoices, including items such as inventory and utility bills are recorded under liabilities.

Putting It All Together

The information sources in the table below will help you develop and finalize your business plan for an accounting service business. Sources for additional information are summarized as follows:

Associations

Association of Bridal Consultants (860) 355-0464; *www.bridalassn.com*

National Bridal Service: (804) 355-6945; *www.nationalbridalservice.com*

Books & Publications

Bridal Bargains, Denise Fields and Alan Fields (Windsor Peak Press, 2002)

The Complete Outdoor Wedding Planner, Sharon Naylor (Prima Lifestyles, 2001)

The Perfect Wedding Reception, Maria McBride-Mellinger (HarperResource, 2000)

Websites

Bride's: (212) 286-2860; *www.brides.com*

Modern Bride: (800) 777-5786; *www.modernbride.com*

On-line courses: *www.elearners.com*

June Wedding Inc. offers courses: (702) 474-9558; *www.junewedding.com*

Financial Consulting

Financial consulting includes several categories of work. You can work as a generalist, providing companies with a wide range of financial services such as developing long-range financial projections and funding requirements, or you can specialize in investment management, capital equipment planning, insurance, or tax management. Use the information and ideas in the following sections to create a financial consulting business plan.

Business Overview

The demand for financial consultants will remain strong among both large and small firms. Despite the desirability of financial planning, only about one-third of Americans prepare a long-term financial plan or use an accountant or financial planner, according to a 2003 Gallup survey. This means that there is a large, untapped market needing the help of a financial consultant. Financial planning includes several categories of work. You can work as a generalist, providing people with a wide range of advisory services such as developing college savings and retirement plans, or you can be a specialist focused on investments, estate planning, wealth management, insurance, or tax reduction.

Financial Consulting Overview			
	Low	**Medium**	**High**
Cost to Start		*	
Operating Costs		*	
Potential Earnings			*
Computer Skills			*
Deadline Pressure	*		
Flexible Schedule		*	
Job Stress		*	

Marketing Financial Consulting

Only one-third of American businesses prepare a long-term financial plan. This means that there is a large untapped market of companies needing the help of a financial consultant. Here's how to tap into that market. The following list will give you some ideas on how to develop a marketing and sales base for a financial consulting business:

- Network inside business and trade organizations such as the chamber of commerce and business referral organizations.

- Obtain referrals and doing overload financial work for CPA and accounting firms. Writing a column or articles for publications and send out your own newsletter. Get listed as a consulting service in referral services that professional associations maintain for their members.

- Create your own website. Without a website, you will not get as many leads from database directories maintained by national organizations that refer consumers seeking a financial consulting. Most "Find a Consultant" directories provide the ability to link the consumer directly to your website. List your business website in directories like *switchboard.com* and *anywho.com.*

- Call on firms in your market area and introduce yourself and your business. Get referrals from business associates to establish a base of clients from which you can use further referrals to expand.

What to Charge

How much should you charge will depend on the geographical area covered by your business? Most independent accountants charge by the hour with fees ranging between $50 and $125 an hour depending on locale and the industries they work in.

Financial Projections

Apply the information in the following financial projection table will help you setup your own financial projections in the templates covered in the Appendix.

Financial Consulting Business Financial Projections	
Funding Requirements	Projecting what you will expend starting up this business should be minimal if you already have the computer equipment you need. If not, include those costs in your funding requirements worksheet.
Income and Expenses	Projected total monthly revenue is subtracted from total monthly expenses to determine if you broke even or made money.
Cash Flow	For new start-ups, the cash flow projections are important because it tells you the times in the year when you can expect a cash surplus and the times when you can expect a cash shortage.
Assets and Liabilities	The total sum of short-term loans due in 60 days or less. The total principal sum of long-term loans owed by the business to banks and investors. Once you have determined your net worth, you will be in a better position to identify the best financial transition into your new business.

Putting It All Together

The information sources in the table below will help you develop and finalize your business plan for a financial consulting business. Sources for additional information are summarized as follows:

Associations

Financial Planning Association (FPATM); (800) 322-4237

National Association of Personal Financial Advisors (NAPFA), (800) 366-2732; *www.napfa.org*

Society of Financial Service Professionals (SFSP): (610) 526-*2500; www.financialpro.org*

Books & Publications

Financial advisors keep up with the popular financial publications like the *Wall Street Journal, Barron's, Forbes, the Economist, Kiplinger's, Personal Finance, Money, Smart Money,* and *Worth*

Websites

American College has a distance education through its American College Online Services: (888) 263-7265; *www.amercoll.edu.*

Certified Financial Planner Board of Standards website site provides a directory of education programs located throughout the United States (888) 237-6275, (303) *830-7500; www.cfp.net.*

College for Financial Planning: (800) 237-9990; *wwwfp.edu*

Financial Planning

Despite the desirability of financial planning, only about ten percent of Americans prepare a long-term financial plan. This means that there is a large, untapped market for financial planners. Financial planning includes several categories of work. You can work as a generalist, providing people with a wide range of advisory services such as developing college savings and retirement plans, or you can be a specialist focusing on investments, estate planning, wealth management, insurance, or tax reduction. Use the information and ideas in the following sections to create a financial planning business plan.

Business Overview

If you're over fifty, you undoubtedly recognize how critical financial planning can be for families and individuals as they grow older. To shine in this business, you need to enjoy working with details and numbers because that's the nature of what you'll be doing, but you need to have sufficient people skills to earn your clients' confidence and trust. You will need access to a car because most daily money managers pick up bills and papers from at least some of their clients and then return checks for them to sign. This level of service distinguishes you from the free or low-cost services available from some local governments and the AARP that have been established to serve low-income individuals.

Depending on which focus you choose, you will benefit from having a certification in financial planning, which you may need a license to practice in your state. However, most states do not have statutes that regulate the qualifications for financial planners. You will have far more credibility if you have specific training and have passed an exam that allows you to call yourself a registered or certified financial consultant or investment advisor.

Financial Planning Overview			
	Low	Medium	High
Cost to Start		*	
Operating Costs		*	
Potential Earnings			*
Computer Skills			*
Deadline Pressure	*		
Flexible Schedule		*	
Job Stress		*	

Marketing Financial Planning

You can specialize your practice to service specific markets or needs, like college planning, premarital planning, tax strategies, and retirement planning to name a few. Communicating to clients about the value of financial planning is best done by using personal stories, metaphors, and analogies. People often can be motivated to recognize the importance of financial planning in their own lives if they hear success and woe stories about others. The following list will give you some ideas on how to develop a marketing and sales base for a financial planning business:

- Get referrals from your family and friends to establish a base of clients from which you can use further referrals to expand. If you plan to have clients come to your home office, you need to make sure your office has the air of a prosperous professional.

- Teach a course at a local community colleges and speak to local organizations such as Kiwanis Clubs, Rotary, and so on. Writing a column or articles for publications or send out your own print newsletter.

- Network with attorneys, accountants, and insurance agents who specialize in estate planning.

- Create your own website. Without a website, you will not get as many leads from database directories maintained by national organizations that refer consumers seeking a financial planning professional. Most "Find a Planner" directories provide the ability to link the consumer directly to your page.

- Get listed as a financial planner in referral services that professional associations maintain for their members. List your business in the Yellow Pages and your website in Web directories like *switchboard.com* and *anywho.com*.

- Often recent widowhood or divorce is the trigger for someone becoming a client.

What to Charge

Typically $25 or $35 an hour, but some daily money managers get as much as $60 an hour. Charging a minimum fee equivalent to two hours a month is not uncommon. To keep your overhead low, establish that expenses like postage, long distance calls made for clients, and mileage are reimbursable. Some daily money managers also charge for travel time. How much should you charge will depend on the geographical area covered by your business? Most independent accountants charge by the hour with fees ranging between $25 and $75 an hour. Some charge below $25, and a few can command more than $75 an hour depending on locale and the industries they work in.

Financial Projections

Apply the information in the following financial projection table will help you setup your own financial projections in the templates covered in the Appendix.

Financial Planning Business Financial Projections	
Funding Requirements	Projecting what you will expend starting up this business should be minimal if you already have the computer equipment you need. If not, include those costs in your funding requirements worksheet.
Income and Expenses	Projected total monthly revenue is subtracted from total monthly expenses to determine how much you plan to make on a per hour basis.
Cash Flow	Knowing what your cash position is enables you to manage your money and it gives you the opportunity to secure working capital funding to avoid running out of cash when you have projected a cash shortage.
Assets and Liabilities	The total sum of short-term loans due in 60 days or less. The total principal sum of long-term loans owed by the business to banks and investors. Once you have determined your net worth, you will be in a better position to identify the best financial transition into your new business.

Putting It All Together

The information sources in the table below will help you develop and finalize your business plan for a financial planning business. Sources for additional information are summarized as follows:

Associations

Financial Planning Association (FPATM); (800) 322-4237 fplannet.org

National Association of Personal Financial Advisors (NAPFA), (800) 366-2732; *www.napfa.org*

Society of Financial Service Professionals (SFSP): (610) 526-*2500; www.financialpro.org*

Books & Publications

Financial planners keep up with the popular financial publications, among them the *Wall Street Journal, Barron's, Forbes, the Economist, Kiplinger's, Personal Finance, Money, Smart Money,* and *Worth*

Websites

American College has a distance education through its American College Online Services: (888) 263-7265; *www.amercoll.edu.*

Certified Financial Planner Board of Standards (CFP®) website site provides a directory of education programs located throughout the United States (888) 237-6275, (303) *830-7500; www.cfp.net.*

Americans need help managing their finances. To learn more about the financial planner business, contact the Financial Planners Association (www.fplanet.org

Fitness Training

You can join the fitness field in any of several ways. You might become a personal trainer, teacher, coach, group motivational speaker, or all of those rolled into one. You can work with clients of all ages and sizes or you can focus on the huge and growing sixty-plus population. Use the information and ideas in the following sections to create a fitness training business plan.

Business Overview

There are several ways to get into the fitness training business. You can become a personal trainer, a fitness teacher, coach, speaker on fitness, or all those things combined. You can choose to work with clients of all sizes and age groups or focus on one particular group like the 60-plus boomers. There is also a ready market for people who are in rehabilitation, and need special help. You can get started by practicing as either a generalists or a specialists in one of several areas; group fitness instruction, water exercise, aerobics, diet and nutrition.

Fitness Training Overview			
	Low	**Medium**	**High**
Cost to Start	*		
Operating Costs	*		
Potential Earnings		*	
Computer Skills		*	
Deadline Pressure		*	
Flexible Schedule		*	
Job Stress		*	

Marketing Fitness Training

Satisfied clients who are anxious to show their friends the progress they've made and are willing to provide referrals are the key to building a busy fitness practice. If your market is glutted with trainers, target your market to a specific group to set yourself apart from the rest. The following list will give you some ideas on how to develop a marketing and sales base for a fitness training business:

- Develop relationships and directly soliciting referrals from chiropractors, orthopedic doctors, and others who have patients that may need the type of fitness training you do.

- Give presentations in the form of seminars, workshops, and speeches where you can demonstrate what you do. Provide handouts that give basic information about fitness training, what you can do, and how to contact you.

- Have a booth at health conventions where you will meet potential clients.

- Have your own Web page with its own domain name with testimonial letters and any articles you have written that identifies what services you offer.

- Participate in community outreach programs, causes, and fund raising events to get your name known.

- Showing your expertise by writing articles and letters to the editors of newspapers and business journals. This can lead to being used as a source by journalists.

- Networking face-to-face inside business and trade organizations such as the chamber of commerce and business referral organizations.

- Obtaining referrals and doing overload work from physical therapy clinics.

What to Charge

How much should you charge will depend on the geographical area covered by your business? Most independent accountants charge by the hour with fees ranging between $25 and $75 an hour. Some charge below $25, and a few can command more than $100 an hour depending on locale and the competition.

Financial Projections

Apply the information in the following financial projection table will help you setup your own financial projections in the templates covered in the Appendix.

Fitness Training Business Financial Projections	
Funding Requirements	How much money is needed to start the business and how will the money is used?
Income and Expenses	Projected total monthly revenue is subtracted from total monthly expenses to determine if you broke even or made money.
Cash Flow	Source of cash usually come from training services. Your use of cash to meet expenses should be minimal for this business.
Assets and Liabilities	The total of loans owed by the business to banks and investors will probably be your major liabilities in this business. Once you have determined your net worth by subtracting total liabilities from total assets, you will be in a better position to identify the best financial transition into your new business.

Putting It All Together

The information sources in the table below will help you develop and finalize your business plan for a fitness training business. Sources for additional information are summarized as follows:

Associations

American Council on Exercise (858) 279-8227 www.acefitness.org
Aerobic and Fitness Association of America (800) 446-2322 www.afaa.com

American Fitness Professionals and Associates (609) 978-7583 www.afpafitness.com

Books & Publications

Start You Own Training Business by Jacquelyn Lynn (Entrepreneur Media, 2003)

Personal Trainer's Handbook by Teri O'Brien (Human Kinetics, 2003)

Websites

Fitness by Phone (www.fitnessbyphone.com) is a website that offers several ideas on communicating with client prospects that are interested in fitness training

Food Catering

Does everyone tell you what a great cook you are? Do you love to cook? If so, you can put these two ingredients together to start a catering business or become a personal chef. You can cater to family or business events or for individual households. They differ from caters in that the cooking is done in their client's home on a scheduled basis. Personal chefs do the grocery shopping and bring their own utensils and equipment with them. They typically cook for their clients once a month and for special occasions like birthday parties and holiday celebrations. Use the information and ideas in the following sections to create a food catering business plan.

Business Overview

The demand for food catering has been steadily increasing over the past 5 years, despite the setbacks in the economy. Although more people are taking gourmet cooking classes and watching the surge in television related programs, not many are actually taking the time out of their busy schedules to prepare special meals. They are willing to hire food caters and personal chefs to do it for them.

Food Catering Overview			
	Low	Medium	High
Cost to Start		*	
Operating Costs	*		
Potential Earnings		*	
Computer Skills			*
Deadline Pressure			*
Flexible Schedule		*	
Job Stress		*	

Marketing Food Catering

The key benefits you offer clients are providing a higher skill level than they can afford to get by hiring a full-time employee. The following list will give you some ideas on how to develop a marketing and sales base for a food catering business:

- Network face-to-face inside business and trade organizations such as the chamber of commerce and business referral organizations. Be prepared to give interested prospects a sample menu or brochure.

- CPA firms and accounting firms are typically overloaded during the tax season and can be excellent sources for you catering services.

- Get listed as a support service in referral services that professional associations maintain for their members.

- Have a website that identifies what services you offer so that potential customers using a search engine will find your site.

- Call on service firms within your market area and introduce yourself and your business.

- List your business in the Yellow Pages and your website in Web directories like *switchboard.com* and *anywho.com*. Consider placing ads on local directory sites like *Yahoo Get Local* and *SuperPages*.

What to Charge

Most caters charge by the hour or by the job. Sometimes they will use a combination of pricing methods depending upon the job. For example, they will charge a flat rate plus so much per person served plus expenses. Pricing by the job accommodates clients who prefer to pay a fixed price.

Financial Projections

Apply the information in the following financial projection table will help you setup your own financial projections in the templates covered in the Appendix.

Food Catering Business Financial Projections	
Funding Requirements	Funding requirements should be broken into two categories; current funding and future funding requirements as is shown in the financial projections shown in the Appendix.
Income and Expenses	Projected total monthly revenue is subtracted from total monthly expenses to determine it you broke even or made money to make on a per hour basis.
Cash Flow	Use of cash is money paid out to cover the expenses of the business that are due in a particular month.
Assets and Liabilities	First, looking at your personal net worth, are you in a financial position to start the business? If you are not financially in a position to start a new business, you must identify how to raise the money needed. s

Putting It All Together

The information sources in the table below will help you develop and finalize your business plan for a food catering business. Sources for additional information are summarized as follows:

Associations

American Personal Chef Association; (800) 644-8389 www.peronalchef.com

United States Personal Chef Association; (800) 995-2138 www.uspca.com

Books & Publications

How to Open and Operate a Home-Based Catering Business by Denise Vivaldo (Globe Pequot Press, 2002)

A Personal Chef Cooks by Cheryl Mochau (First Book Library, 2003)

Websites

Personal Catering Business; www.mymommybiz.com

Handyman Services

In the life of any house, there comes a time for remodeling, but in between, before that time comes, there are a lot of little jobs that are too small for a professional contractor and too much for the busy homeowner. This is where the handyman (or woman) comes in. From adjusting a leaky faucet to putting a closet door back on the rail, doing odd jobs for homeowners can be a great business that will keep you as busy as you want to be. It requires some skill and know-how with tools, so if you have been fixing things around your own house for years and enjoy a variety of small jobs that can be finished quickly, offering handyman services could be an enjoyable full-time or part-time business for you. Use the information and ideas in the following sections to create a handyman services business plan.

Business Overview

Over time, every house will need to be remodeled or undergo some repairs. This is where the handyman or handywoman comes in. From remodeling a bathroom to fixing a leaking faucet, doing odd jobs for busy homeowners can become a great startup business that will keep you as busy as you want to be.

Handyman Services Overview			
	Low	Medium	High
Cost to Start		*	
Operating Costs		*	
Potential Earnings		*	
Computer Skills	*		
Deadline Pressure		*	
Flexible Schedule	*		
Job Stress		*	

Marketing Handyman Services

The key benefits you offer clients are availability and being less expensive than trade personnel.

Trust is fundamental to this business. "There are not a lot of handymen around that people feel they can trust," state both Alonzo and Peterson. Customers need to be able to leave you a list and the key and know the job will be done and their house will be standing when they get back.

As a handyman, you may find yourself doing almost anything you're willing to do, including hanging wallpaper, painting, installing flooring, electrical wiring, fixing decking, repairing roofs, cleaning gutters, and replacing tiles. You need to have all the tools required to do whatever services you provide. You should also carry small supplies like Spackle or the odd bolt just to save time and trips to and from the hardware store, but it's acceptable and probably good practice to have your customer purchase major materials like gallons of paint and significant plumbing parts.

Referrals are the number-one way to build a clientele and even if your work is satisfactory, people need to trust you to refer others to you. Give yourself time to develop a sufficient number of customers so that you're turning down work instead of looking for it. Dressing presentably and neatly separates you from the workers people are suspicious of when they see them in their neighborhoods. Because people feel pride in their homes, complimenting their house helps establish rapport. The following list will give you some ideas on how to develop a marketing and sales base for a handyman services business:

- Make yourself indispensable to someone with a fixer-upper is one way to stay busy for several months or even years. Let people know what you are doing in your personal circles.

- Solicit businesses in condominium complexes as often the owners don't have tools and equipment to do home improvement and repairs.

- Call on real estate offices and leaving fliers.

- Advertise in local shopper papers and post fliers, cards, and brochures on community bulletin boards.

- Have attractive signage on your truck or vehicle with your phone number and website visible.

- Offer short courses on fixing household items through local adult-education programs.

- If you live in or near a resort area where people have second homes, soliciting absent owners for off-season work.

- Network inside business and trade organizations such as the chamber of commerce.

- Create a website that identifies what services you offer so that potential customers using a search engine will find your site.

- Call on hardware and home furnishing stores in your market area and introduce yourself and your business.

- List your business in the Yellow Pages and your website in directories like *switchboard.com* and *anywho.com*.

What to Charge

A rule of thumb is two-thirds the rates of plumbers and electricians, whose overhead costs are higher. There's a large variation from $15 an hour in low-cost areas to $80 an hour major metropolitan areas. The rate for emergency or after-hours service may be up to double the regular hourly rate.

How much should you charge will depend on the geographical area covered by your business? Most independent accountants charge by the hour with fees ranging between $25 and $75 an hour. Some charge below $25, and a few can command more than $75 an hour depending on locale and the industries they work in.

Financial Projections

Apply the information in the following financial projection table will help you setup your own financial projections in the templates covered in the Appendix.

Handyman Services Business Financial Projections	
Funding Requirements	Projecting what you will expend starting up your business is a critical component of the startup process.
Income and Expenses	Projected total monthly revenue is subtracted from total monthly expenses to determine if you broke even or made money.
Cash Flow	The cash flow projection shows how money will flow into your business in the form of revenues and flow out of the business in the form of expenses to make on a per hour basis.
Assets and Liabilities	First, looking at your personal net worth, are you in a financial position to start the business? If you are not financially in a position to start a new business, you must identify how to raise the money needed.

Putting It All Together

The information sources in the table below will help you develop and finalize your business plan for a handyman services business. Sources for additional information are summarized as follows:

Associations

Association of Certified Handyman Professionals; www.achpnet.org

Books & Publications

Handyman's Handbook by David Koenigsberg (McGraw-Hill Professional, 2003)

Buy It, Fix It, and Sell It by Kevin C. Myers (Dearborn Trade Publishing, 1997)

Websites

House Doctors Handyman Service: (800) 319-3359, (513) 831-*0100*
www.housedoctors.com

Guide and CDs: *www.handyman-business.com*

Natural Handyman: *www.naturalhandyman.com*

Home Inspections

Home inspection got its start in the 1970s when mortgage institutions wanted to verify that the properties on which they were about to make loans on were a good risk. The demand grew for home inspection after states like California passed laws requiring sellers to disclose any existing problems with their home to prospective buyers, placing liability on the seller and real estate agents, too.

The home inspector objectively examines a residence to identify its structural soundness and the quality of all its systems. The goals are to detect any signs of failure, safety problems, or wear and tear, and to estimate the remaining useful life of the home's major systems and finishes. Formerly done by visual inspection, today's inspectors may use high-tech tools to examine the roof, foundation, attic, insulation, walkways, heating, air conditioning, plumbing, and electrical systems.

Often these reports play an important role in the sale of the home. If defects are found, the buyer may choose to accept the problems, obtain a larger mortgage to pay for fixing the problems, renegotiate the offer to make the seller correct the problems, or even decline the purchase. When working for the seller, the inspector's analysis can help the homeowner become aware of any defects that could affect the home's price or that might cause a deal to fall through. Use the information and ideas in the following sections to create a home inspections business plan.

Business Overview

Most new home inspectors have a background in the construction industry or in the maintenance field. Often inspectors are people who became tired of wearing a belt or have been injured on the job and need to do less strenuous work. Getting into this field requires extensive up-to-date knowledge about home construction, building codes, and all the systems in a house. You can't have a fear of heights or claustrophobia, because you will need to go up on roofs and in crawl spaces beneath homes.

Working as an inspector requires errors-and-omissions insurance to cover potential liability for oversights and mistakes. This will be difficult to obtain until you have passed the ASHI test, but once you have, you will be able to purchase it through the association. Be aware that the profession is saturated in some major cities, but the field will likely grow in regions where the population is expanding. Although there are no laws requiring a home inspection, it is estimated that roughly 70 percent of homes sold are inspected, making home inspections almost as common as termite inspections.

You can determine whether your state currently requires a license for home inspectors along with a summary of the regulatory legislation on the ASHI website (*ashi.comlinspectorslstate.htm*). If you have construction experience and are prepared to invest some time and money in a training program that will qualify you as a home inspector, then this may be a good opportunity for you. Contact the National Association of Home inspectors (www.nahi.org) to learn more.

Home Inspections Overview			
	Low	**Medium**	**High**
Cost to Start	*		
Operating Costs	*		
Potential Earnings			*
Computer Skills		*	
Deadline Pressure	*		
Flexible Schedule		*	
Job Stress	*		

Marketing Home Inspections

An excellent growth area for inspections is new construction. Although you might not think brand-new homes need an inspection, buyers today are wary of new construction, no doubt due to hearing horror stories about dissatisfied home buyers forced to sue home builders. Although contractors are required to have a city building inspector check their work at every major stage, the city inspectors are not as rigorous as home inspectors and they don't represent the buyer. As a result, many buyers of new homes bring in their own inspectors to confirm good-quality construction. The following list will give you some ideas on how to develop a marketing and sales base for a home inspections business:

- Meet real estate agents at open houses and at industry-related business groups, such as the Board of Realtors, Women's Councils of Realtors, as well as business-referral organizations.

- Introduce yourself at weekly meetings before caravans (when agents go see properties that have been newly listed for sale). Anytime you can provide high-quality information face-to-face you will be appreciated. Getting in good with a popular agent in one office can set you up for many inspections.

- Give lectures and training in real estate offices on topics such as how not to let inspection kill your deal and new areas of concern.

- Join the American Society of Home Inspectors (ASHI), which refers potential clients to its members and has a "Find an Inspector" service on its website.

- Have your own website and link it to ASHI's website for listings.

- Join your state or local chapter of home inspectors. If you specialize in the type of home inspection you do, you may develop referral relationships with other inspectors.

- Obtain publicity in real estate sections of the newspaper and then using reprints in your promotional and sales materials to establish credibility.

What to Charge

The fee for a home inspection varies by region. In most cases, the fee ranges from $225 to $400, with $250 to $300 being the average in urban areas. Rural areas are lower. It takes about two hours to complete an inspection, plus additional time to write the report. Note: A busy inspector can do 200 to 250 inspections per year, averaging about one inspection a day.

Financial Projections

Apply the information in the following financial projection table will help you setup your own financial projections in the templates covered in the Appendix.

Home Inspections Business Financial Projections	
Funding Requirements	Projecting what you will expend starting up your business is a critical component of the startup process.
Income and Expenses	Projected total monthly revenue is subtracted from total monthly expenses to determine it you broke even or made money to make on a per hour basis.
Cash Flow	The cash flow projection is important because it can tell you the times during the year when you can expect a cash surplus and the times in the year when you can expect a cash shortage.
Assets and Liabilities	The balance sheet lists the cash value of your assets and liabilities. Total liabilities are subtracted from the total value of your assets to determine your net worth or equity position in your business.

Putting It All Together:

The information sources in the table below will help you develop and finalize your business plan for a home inspections business. Sources for additional information are summarized as follows:

Associations

American Society of Home Inspectors (ASHI) (800) 743-2744, (847) 759-2820 *www.ashi.com*

National Association of Home Inspectors (NAHI) (800) 448-3942 (952) 928-4641 *www.nahi.org*

Books & Publications

Become A *Home Inspector!* Michael A. Pompeii (Pompeii Books & Publications, 2001)

Home Inspection Handbook, John E. Traister (Craftsman House, 1997)

The Home Inspection Troubleshooter, Robert Irwin (Dearborn Publishing, 1995)

Websites

Home inspection training systems;
www.homeinspection@dearborne.com

Inspection Training Associates; (800) 323-9235 www.home-inspection.com

Home Security

Home security is one of the fastest-growing segments of the home services and products industry. It offers a number of related startup opportunities, such as sales and installations of window security bars and shutters, home alarm sales and installations, and the latest in closed-circuit surveillance cameras to name a few. The latest trends require a technical know-how, especially for high-end systems. Therefore, unless you have an extensive background in the security field, you will need to take training classes in all the latest crime deterrents. Contact the International Association of Professional Security Consultants (www.iapsc.org) to learn more.

Use the information and ideas in the following sections to create a home security business plan.

Business Overview

Most new home security specialists have a background in the military, law enforcement, or in corporate security. Often security specialists are people who want to work with others to improve their safety and well-being. Getting into this field requires extensive up-to-date knowledge about home construction, building codes, and the latest in home security systems. The home security specialists objectively examine a residence to identify its security soundness and the quality of all its systems. The goals are to detect any signs of safety problems and to estimate the remaining useful life of the home's existing security systems. First-rate computer skills are vital, as are creativity and intuition when it comes to researching the latest developments on home security systems.

Home Security Overview			
	Low	**Medium**	**High**
Cost to Start	*		
Operating Costs	*		
Potential Earnings			*
Computer Skills		*	
Deadline Pressure	*		
Flexible Schedule		*	
Job Stress	*		

Marketing Home Security

An excellent growth area for home security specialists is new construction. Although you might not think brand-new homes need a security inspection, buyers today are wary of break-in to new homes, no doubt due to hearing horror stories about forced break-ins that appear in the newspapers daily. As a result, many buyers of new homes are anxious to bring in their security specialists to confirm the safety of their new home. The following list will give you some ideas on how to develop a marketing and sales base for a home security business:

- Meet real estate agents at open houses and at industry-related business groups, such as the Board of Realtors, Women's Councils of Realtors, as well as business-referral organizations.

- Introduce yourself at weekly meetings before caravans (when agents go see properties that have been newly listed for sale). Anytime you can provide high-quality information face-to-face you will be appreciated. Getting in good with a popular agent in one office can set you up for many inspections.

- Give lectures and training in real estate offices on topics such as how not to let safety concerns kill their deal.

- Join the International Association of Professional Security Consultants - APSC (www.iapsc.org), which refers potential clients to its members.

- Have your own website and link it to APSC's website for client referrals.

- Obtain publicity in real estate sections of the newspaper and then using reprints in your promotional and sales materials to establish credibility.

- Have a booth at home and garden shows conventions where you will meet potential clients.

- List in the Yellow Pages is helpful for reaching the general public about your work but not for corporate work.

- Show your expertise by writing articles and letters to the editors of newspapers and business journals. This can lead to being used as a source by journalists.

What to Charge

How much should you charge will depend on the geographical area covered by your business? Most home security consultants charge by the hour with fees ranging between $25 and $75 an hour. Some charge below $25, and a few can command more than $75 an hour depending on locale and the industries they work in.

Financial Projections

Apply the information in the following financial projection table will help you setup your own financial projections in the templates covered in the Appendix.

Home Security Business Financial Projections	
Funding Requirements	Projecting what you will expend starting up your business is a critical component of the startup process.
Income and Expenses	Projected total monthly revenue is subtracted from total monthly expenses to determine it you broke even or made money to make on a per hour basis.
Cash Flow	The cash flow projection shows how money will flow into the business in the form of cash and flow out of the business for paid expenses usually monthly.
Assets and Liabilities	Knowing what your personal financial situation is (i.e., net worth) on a monthly basis important because it will enable you to determine how you business is doing financially over time.

Putting It All Together

The information sources in the table below will help you develop and finalize your business plan for a home security business. Sources for additional information are summarized as follows:

Associations

International Association of Professional Security Consultants (www.iapsc.org)

National Association of Home Inspectors (NAHI) (800) 448-3942 (952) 928-4641 *www.nahi.org*

Books & Publications

Become A Home Inspector! by Michael A. Pompeii (Pompeii Books & Publications, 2001)

Home Inspection Handbook by John E. Traister (Craftsman House, 1997)

The Home Inspection Troubleshooter by Robert Irwin (Dearborn Publishing, 1995)

Websites

The Home Security Store website features an array of home security products; (888) 501-7870 www.homesecuritystore.com

Instructor Sessions

Specialized instruction is one of the best home businesses to start because in most cases, the product (your skill) helps others learn more about something that interest them and improve themselves in the process. Capitalize on your knowledge and experience by starting a home based instruction business. Depending on your skills, you could offer classes on cooking, gardening, home improvement, dog training, self defense, survival, music lessons, languages, sewing or anything you have mastered yourself. You will need to create a lesson plan, decide on how many students you can accommodate (e.g., in your home or in a rented space). Decide on the level of the instruction-beginning, intermediate or advanced. Contact the National Tutoring Association (ntatutor.org) to learn more. Use the information and ideas in the following sections to create an instructor sessions business plan.

Business Overview

In a little more than a decade, instructor specialists have emerged as a distinct profession, attracting baby boomers into the profession. Most baby boomers have acquired years of knowledge on how to play the game of life – how to make the right decisions and avoid making the wrong decisions along the way. Offering specialized instruction has evolved into a lucrative startup business where boomers are offering their experience for a fee to clients in group settings. If you like to work with people in training and the consulting environment, then there are lots of opportunities for you to explore.

Instructor specialists typically specialize on career transitions, creativity, quality of life, health, and wellness, professional development, relationships, finances, balancing work with life, to name some of the common specialties. You need strong interpersonal skills to succeed in this business. You may decide to work with companies who want you to instruct their employees on issues such as business planning, personal financing, strategic planning, conflict management, team building, partnership relations, and productivity.

Instructor Sessions Overview			
	Low	**Medium**	**High**
Cost to Start	*		
Operating Costs	*		
Potential Earnings			*
Computer Skills			*
Deadline Pressure		*	
Flexible Schedule		*	
Job Stress		*	

Marketing Instructor Sessions

There is a vast market for instructor specialists because many people simply prefer specialized instruction on a specific subject that they are keenly interested in. Identify one or more niches or specializations that will help you attract clients. Ones based on your industry experience or extracurricular interests may offer you immediate contacts with potential clients. The best revenue streams are group coaching and corporate contracts for group sessions with their employees in workshop settings. The key benefit you offer clients is providing them with a high quality instruction. The following list will give you some ideas on how to develop a marketing and sales base for an instructor sessions business:

- Post flyers on bulletin boards throughout your community.

- Write articles for community publications on topics that relate to your subject with your photo and byline, including how to contact you.

- Have a website on which you post testimonial letters from past clients. Be sure to place the name of the community or communities you serve on your home page. List your business in Web directories like *switchboard.com* and *anywho.com.*

- Offer free thirty-minute consultations to client prospects in demo group meetings.

- Make yourself visible by networking in organizations where you are likely to meet people wanting to change or grow.

- Have a website that tells your specialization and approach along with client endorsements.

- Get listed in directories like *findacoach.com* and the International Coach Federation's Coach Referral Service.

- Speak before groups, giving workshops and seminars.

- Write articles about coaching for print and electronic publications, such as newsletters.

- The best referrals come from your own clients who become your evangelists. Most likely clients are people in some form of transition, typically between the ages of thirty-five and fifty-five.

- Network face-to-face inside business and trade organizations such as the chamber of commerce and business referral organizations.

What to Charge

How much should you charge will depend on the geographical area covered by your business? Most instructor specialists charge their clients by the hour with fees ranging between $25 to $70 an hour or session. A few can command more than $70 an hour depending on locale and their area of specialization.

Financial Projections

Apply the information in the following financial projection table will help you setup your own financial projections in the templates covered in the Appendix.

Instructor Sessions Business Financial Projections	
Funding Requirements	How much money is needed to start the business and how will the money be used?
Income and Expenses	Projected total monthly revenue is subtracted from total monthly expenses to determine if you broke even or made money.
Cash Flow	For new start-ups, the cash flow projections are important because it tells you the times in the year when you can expect a cash surplus and the times when you can expect a cash shortage to make on a per hour basis.
Assets and Liabilities	The balance sheet lists the cash value of your assets and liabilities. Total liabilities are subtracted from the total value of your assets to determine your net worth or equity position in your business.

Putting It All Together

The information sources in the table below will help you develop and finalize your business plan for an instructor sessions business. Sources for additional information are summarized as follows:

Associations

The International Coach Federation (ICF): (888) 423-3131, *www.coachfederation.org*

Books & Publications

Coaching with Spirit by Teri Belf (Jossey-Bass/Pfeiffer, 2002)

Getting Started in Personal and Executive Coaching by Stephen Fairley and Chris Stout (John Wiley & Sons, 2003)

Leading High Impact Teams: The Coach Approach to Peak Performance by Cynder Niemela and Rachael Lewis (High Impact Pub, 2001)

Personal and Executive Coaching by Jeffrey Auerbach (Executive College Press, 2001)

Websites

See a list comparing the many coaching schools at *www.coachingschools.org*

Coach University, *www.coachu.com* or (800) 48COACH, (604)990-3545

Academy for Coach Training: *www.coachtraining.com*

Internet and Blogging Sales

Literally millions of people make millions of dollars every day selling their products and services on the Internet. It's not easy, but if you know what you're doing, you too can make money selling on the Internet.

Today, more and more people are shopping online and there are more e-retailers popping up every day. Your primary weapon against the competition is having a great-looking website with great content. Search engine optimization (keyword placement, link campaigns, and pertinent content) helps your search rankings. Good product descriptions and professional-looking photos enhance the credibility of your website.

There is an online business called blogging that doesn't require you to sell products where you writing information on a website that people want. Blogging is a viable business that can generate thousands in advertising revenue. There are thousands of bloggers out there, but the top bloggers in the field today didn't exist three years ago. All you need for success in this business is an Internet connection and a great idea. How much revenue you generate depends on the size and desirability of your audience to advertisers. For example, if you manage to create a very popular blog about what car to buy, the world's automakers will race to advertise on your site. U.S. online advertising has grown to $27 billion industry or about 10 percent of total U.S. advertising spending. Use the information and ideas in the following sections to create an Internet and blogging sales business plan

Business Overview

Sales over the Internet keep bounding upward as busy schedules and the search for great bargains attract increasing numbers of people shopping on the Internet. Many home businesses are using *eBay* to sell their goods. If you have products to market, then you can make the world your market on the Internet. There are two primary approaches to selling on the Internet. One is to operate a virtual storefront on a website where you showcase your products. The other way to sell products on the Internet is through hitchhiking onto auction sites like *eBay, Yahoo Auction,* and *Amazon.com Auctions.* They have the largest auction site, which has become a primary or supplementary way to sell your wares to all kinds of people.

As a seller on an auction site, you pay the site a fee to list your product. The site acts as an electronic intermediary but never actually handles your products. *EBay* works well for so many people because it enables sellers to operate with little overhead and to get a volume of sales one could only otherwise expect in a high-rent, highly trafficked commerce allocation. When selling at auction sites, you do not have to maintain a website or a database. You simply follow the auction's site instructions to sell anything from antique cars to vintage clothing to used CDs and almost anything you can think of, including yachts, islands, and ferry boats. Not that there's no work involved-you have to create listings to describe your products, manage your inventory, track your sales, and satisfy your customers.

If you decide to start an Internet blogging business, it has to be about a something people will want to read. Think about what expertise or point of view you can bring to the uninformed. If you specialize in a specific area of knowledge, write about it. Surf the sites you normally would and when you find something interesting, link to it in your blog and make a short comment about it. You are telling your blog's readers that this news item you've found is worth their time.

Internet and Blogging Sales Overview			
	Low	Medium	High
Cost to Start		*	
Operating Costs		*	
Potential Earnings			*
Computer Skills			*
Deadline Pressure		*	
Flexible Schedule	*		
Job Stress		*	

Marketing Internet and Blogging Sales

Marketing your product can be done by building awareness of your website, developing good customer service, and finding every opportunity to place your product in the public light. Search engine optimization increases your ranking in a search engine result. If you increase the potential customer's chance of accessing your website, then you increase your product's visibility. Make sure that your product descriptions are interesting and that they accurately represent the product. A clearly written description and a professional-looking product photo convey the message that your site is a serious online retail business, not just some mom-and-pop website.

Gathering information about sales trends, product development, customer needs, and purchasing patterns is an important part of your Internet business activities. Knowing this will help you understand the various factors that affect your business. There are a variety of programs and services out there that can track your website traffic, customer purchase patterns, and returns. You can also encourage your customers to e-mail their opinion about the product and the website so that you can know what they're thinking.

Establishing a good blogging website is done through content, the proper mix of graphics, photographs, with well-written information about what you're blogging. A synergy between high-quality graphics and good descriptive content are essential to the contents of your site. Remember that you are creating this site to make money

111

by showcasing your products and services. Part of your sales hook is giving the customer as much content as possible about the products and services you're selling without overloading them. Your graphics might be aesthetically appealing, but if it doesn't relate to what you're selling, it serves no purpose in the content of your site.

Customer input is valuable, especially in online retailing because person-to-person interaction is practically nonexistent. When you begin your Internet and blogging sales business, sales will initially be slow and you'll have the time to monitor your customers' sales patterns. However, as your sales increase, there are programs that you can buy to track your website traffic. These programs can also track what your customers are buying. Tracking your customers' buying behavior lets you know which products are selling and which price points are amenable to your customers. The following list will give you some ideas on how to develop a marketing and sales base for an Internet and blogging sales business:

- List your business in the Yellow Pages and your website in Web directories like *switchboard.com* and *anywho.com.* When you choose a domain name for your website, keep in mind that most people are bad typists so the more character you add to your domain name, the more difficult it will be for customers to enter it and remember it as well.

- Be specific in describing what you are selling and whenever possible, include a good photograph. If you are selling something used, candidly describe any flaws or blemishes.

- If you're auctioning goods, set a low initial bid so that a buyer must meet or exceed a minimum price. Make the auction period cover a weekend when traffic is highest.

- Convenience and lower prices drive shopping on the Web. Convenience translates into speed of service and ease in buying.

- Offer prompt customer service, including answering emails from prospective buyers immediately is vital. Delays in answering, shipping, or resolving problems mean a customer will buy elsewhere or not return. Happy customers will be repeat customers.

- The reputation indicated in the ratings on *eBay*, which comes from customer feedback, will make or break an *eBay* seller's business. This is customer service again. Build up your feedback rating as soon as possible.

- Not everything sells on *eBay* or other auction sites. One of the best ways you find this out is to test promotional strategies and pricing on your own site. Drop whatever doesn't sell.

- If you are selling from your own website, invest time in researching keyword combinations as they are how someone using a search engine will find you.

- Have a bargain section on your website offering a percent discount to buyers. Keep in contact with customers, notifying them of sales, promotions, and special newsletters.

- If auctioning goods, setting a low initial bid and not using a reserve, which means a buyer must meet or exceed a minimum price. Make the auction period cover a weekend when traffic is highest.

- A good blogging website is easy to navigate and is search engine friendly. A websites done strictly in graphic pizzazz that does not give customers what they need to know won't work.

- Be quite specific in describing what you are blogging and include applicable photographs.

What to Charge

Lower prices stand at the top or close to the top of every survey asking people why they shop on the Web. Yet many sellers have found they get better prices than they would get if they sold their wares locally. In the course of doing what they do, auction sites provide an efficient mechanism for finding the price that the market will bear. Many sellers on auction sites shoot for a 100 percent markup, but the key to this is what they pay for what they sell. Another way to receive payment, particularly when you're getting started with your own storefront or on-line catalogue is to use a payment service, like *catalog.com.* Payment services technically resell your products because merchant account agreements do not allow accepting credit cards for another company.

Offer prompt customer service, including answering emails from prospective buyers immediately, is vital. Delays in answering, shipping, or resolving problems mean a customer will buy elsewhere or not return. Happy customers will be repeat customers, which will drive business to advertise on your website.

Financial Projections

Apply the information in the following financial projection table will help you setup your own financial projections in the templates covered in the Appendix.

Internet and Blogging Business Financial Projections	
Funding Requirements	Funding requirements should be broken into two categories; current funding and future funding requirements as is shown in the financial projections in the Appendix.
Income and Expenses	Projected total monthly revenue is subtracted from total monthly expenses to determine if you broke even or made money.

Cash Flow	Knowing what your cash position is enables you to manage your money and it gives you the opportunity to secure working capital funding to avoid running out of cash when you have projected a cash shortage.
Assets and Liabilities	The balance sheet lists the cash value of your assets and liabilities. Total liabilities are subtracted from the total value of your assets to determine your net worth or equity position in your business.

Putting It All Together

The information sources in the table below will help you develop and finalize your business plan for an Internet & blogging sales business. Sources for additional information are summarized as follows:

Associations

Web Marketing Association, www.webmarketingassociation.org

Books & Publications

eBay for Dummies, Marsha Collier (Wiley Books & Publications, 2002)

Secrets of Blogging to a Six-Figure Income by Darren Rouse (Wiley Books & Publications, 2010)

Internal Riches: The Simple Money-Making Secrets of Online Millionaires by Scott Fox (AMACOM, 2008)

Blogging For Dummies by Susannah Graham (Wiley Books & Publications, 2010)

Websites

Ebay.com is the official website for the EBay Company

Landscaping Services

Gardening is the number-one hobby in the United States. Yet as much as everyone loves green lawns and blooming plants, many find gardening and landscaping onerous work or don't have the time to do it. So they would rather hire someone to provide this service for them who is knowledgeable and that they can count on. So if you enjoy gardening and have a green thumb instead of a brown one, you can join the many boomers who are turning their hobby into a home based business. Use the information and ideas in the following to create a landscaping services business plan.

Business Overview

Depending on the climate where you live, this can be a year-round or seasonal business lasting from spring to early winter. Depending on how much you are willing to devote to learning about landscape design methods, you can expand lawn maintenance into custom design. Anyone who enjoys making things grow, has a customer orientation, and is in good enough physical condition to do what's required can provide landscaping services.

Landscaping Services Overview			
	Low	Medium	High
Cost to Start		*	
Operating Costs		*	
Potential Earnings		*	
Computer Skills	*		
Deadline Pressure		*	
Flexible Schedule	*		
Job Stress	*		

Marketing Landscaping Services

The types of services you can offer range from simple maintenance to landscape design and installation. Many customers just want basic maintenance, raking up leaves, cutting grass, clipping hedges, and some pruning. Personal attention, a reputation for reliability, and expert advice cause customers to choose self-employed gardeners over larger services. Word-of-mouth referrals are key to growing a gardening service. Specialization possibilities include focusing on a particular plant species like trees or roses, sustainable plantings, irrigation, and outdoor lighting design and installation.

It's important to guarantee plants you install. Depending on the type of plant, the replacement period can run from six weeks to six months and be from 50 to 100 percent of the replacement cost of the plant. If you buy plants from a wholesaler, chances are the wholesaler rather than you will absorb the cost of the replacement plant. The following list will give you some ideas on how to develop a marketing and sales base for a landscaping services business:

- Face-to-face networking within your industry in organizations related to gardening, grounds management, and maintenance organizations. Get with other gardeners. Larger companies will refer jobs for services they don't provide, particularly if the job is too small or it's a specialized service you do.

- Placing a tasteful contractor sign indicating your name and contact information on your job sites, with the permission of your customer.

- Have a website listing your services with client endorsements.

- Advertise in local papers and offer discounts for first-time customers. Post fliers at garden centers.

- Network face-to-face inside business and trade organizations such as the chamber of commerce and business referral organizations.

- Get listed as a support service in referral services that local associations and organizations maintain for their members.

- Have a website that identifies what services you offer so that potential customers using a search engine will find your site.

- Call on retail stores and commercial firms within your market area that have landscaping on their property and introduce yourself and your business.

- List your business in the Yellow Pages and your website in Web directories like *switchboard.com* and *anywho.com*.

What to Charge

Landscaping service charges go for between $20 to $75 an hour, depending on your market. Installation and maintenance work is about half the landscaping consulting rate. If installation is involved, the design may be free. For customers who want consistent, weekly or monthly service, it's better to provide a flat rate. Hourly rates typically run from $15 to $30.

Financial Projections

Apply the information in the following financial projection table will help you setup your own financial projections in the templates covered in the Appendix.

Landscaping Services Business Financial Projections	
Funding Requirements	Projecting what you will expend starting up your business is a critical component of the startup process.
Income and Expenses	Projected total monthly revenue is subtracted from total monthly expenses to determine if you broke even or made money.

Cash Flow	Source of cash usually come from product and service sales. , use of cash to meet expenses, and remaining cash, which is the total source of cash for each month.
Assets and Liabilities	The balance sheet lists your assets and liabilities, allowing you to determine what your net worth or equity position is in the business. Assets are items that your business owns that have a cash value. Liabilities are debts that your business owes. Your net worth is the difference between the two.

Putting It All Together

The information sources in the table below will help you develop and finalize your business plan for a landscaping services business. Sources for additional information are summarized as follows:

Associations

Associated Landscape Contractors of America offers a certified landscape program: (800) 395-ALCA, (703) 736-9666; *www.alca.org.*

Books & Publications

Making Gardens Works of Art, Keeyla Meadows, (Sasquatch Books & Publications, 2002)

Small Spaces, Beautiful Gardens, Keith Davitt (Rockport Publishers, 2002)

Websites

Lowes' website offers landscaping how-to information with top gardening products. www.lows.com

Mail Order Sales

Mail order is a broad category that can encompass any number of products. Mail order sales remain one of the best opportunities for a home based business. More and more people are shopping from the comfort of their homes, via catalogs, calling toll-free numbers and websites. You want to select products that have high profit margins, are easy to ship, and have mass appeal within a niche target market. You can reach your target audience for your products by launching a direct mail campaign. USA.com (infousa.com) is one of the largest suppliers of mailing lists, which are indexed by consumer, business, industry, hobby interests, geographic and demographic classifications. Contact the National Mail Order Association (www.nmoa.org) to learn more mail order selling. Use the information and ideas in the following sections to create a mail order sales business plan.

Business Overview

Your daily email probably surpasses the letters you receive for ordering all kinds of products, but your mail box may still be crammed with direct mail. Most of it comes from large mailing operations like Omaha Streak enticing you to order their products by direct mail. So is there anything left a home-based mail order business?

Large mailing houses often don't handle untrue and specialty items, so a home-based is sometimes the only that people have purchase products that are not available through the Web or large corporate mailing houses. Often you can draw on your experience in whatever field you've been working. Having had a career in a specialized technical field, for example, might help in developing a specialty in investigating product liability cases; accounting in divorce and forensic work; a background in an art field could be useful working with museums in art-theft prevention. First-rate computer skills are vital, as are creativity and intuition when it comes to knowing how to develop leads for a case.

Mail Order Sales Overview			
	Low	Medium	High
Cost to Start		*	
Operating Costs		*	
Potential Earnings		*	
Computer Skills			*
Deadline Pressure		*	
Flexible Schedule		*	
Job Stress		*	

Marketing Mail Orders

A background in marketing and sales are essential to running a successful direct mail business. Your success will be directly dependent on your ability to create a mailing list of customers that need and want whatever you're selling. In particular, you must have the ability to pay attention to detail and a willingness to learn everything you can about your target market. The following list will give you some ideas on how to develop a marketing and sales base for a mail order business:

- Talk to anybody you can who is already involved in direct mailing to learn how they developed their respective mailing lists.

- Contact companies that sell mailing list and find out what parameters they use in the respective lists that they sell.

- Prepare a marketing questionnaire that will help you identify attributes of your target market. Issues to address in your questionnaire are age, sex, income levels, family status (i.e., single, married), and personal needs.

- Test the questions in your marketing questionnaire by soliciting response, ideas, and criticism from your friends and associates before you send it out.

- Have a booth at conventions of industries you know about or wish to work in where you will meet potential corporate clients.

- Have your own Web page with its own domain name with testimonial letters and any articles you have written. Have a website that identifies what services you offer so that potential customers using a search engine will find your site. Have a website that identifies what services you offer so that potential customers using a search engine will find your site.

What to Charge

How much should you charge for the products you sell in a mail order business? Most retail stores apply a 100 percent markup their product that they sell. An item that cost them one dollar is sold for two dollars. Use that as a "rule of thumb" for the pricing of your mail order products. You obviously have more downward flexibility on price since your overhead costs are substantially less than what retail stores must absorb.

Financial Projections

Apply the information in the following financial projection table will help you setup your own financial projections in the templates covered in the Appendix.

Mail Order Business Financial Projections	
Funding Requirements	How much money is needed to start the business and how will the money is used?
Income and Expenses	Projected total monthly revenue is subtracted from total monthly expenses to determine if you broke even or made money.
Cash Flow	The cash flow projection is important because it can tell you the times during the year when you can expect a cash surplus and the times in the year when you can expect a cash shortage when you acquire inventory.
Assets and Liabilities	Assets are items that your business owns that have value, liabilities are debts that your business owes. The purpose of the balance sheet is to paint a picture of what your business is worth.

Putting It All Together

The information sources in the table below will help you develop and finalize your business plan for a mail order business. Sources for additional information are summarized as follows:

Associations

National Mail Order Association (www.nmoa.org)

Mailing and Fulfillment Association (800) 333-6272 www.masa.org

Books & Publications

Start Your Own Mail Order Business by Rich Mintzer (Entrepreneur Press, 2008)

Websites

The United States postal Service's website provides publications, mailing tips, and software tools (www.usps.com/ncsc)

Management Consulting

If you have prior executive management experience as a CEO, COO, CFO or other leadership role, your next job may literally be right around the corner. Thousands of companies are seeking out ex-executives as consultants. Such executives are in demand for their expertise and experience. Management consultants may be hired to:

- Bring new creativity and innovation into a company

- Getting stalled projects off the ground

- Act as additional manpower during unexpected surges in business

- Realign corporate strategy and bring costs under control

- Contribute to unsolved technical problems

- Teach in-house people a technology or expertise they don't have

In the past, retired executives and professionals were often sidelined because corporations believed the "old folks "were not able to keep up with changing technologies or new business strategies. However, more and more organizations are recognizing that today's older workers have valuable skills to offer and often understand the leading edge of technologies better than many of their current employees. Use the information and ideas in the following sections to create a management consulting business plan.

Business Overview

Management consulting requires significant prior experience in an executive position. You must also have the skills to quickly understand issues and blend in with your client's culture and environment so permanent staff members don't see you as a threat. Though some interim executives over the age of fifty use this path as a way to land new corporate jobs, many of them simply prefer the flexibility and variety that management consulting offers. So, if you are interested in helping a company for a few months without the security of a golden handshake at the end of the path, this work could be your next best move.

Management Consulting Overview			
	Low	**Medium**	**High**
Cost to Start	*		
Operating Costs	*		
Potential Earnings			*
Computer Skills		*	
Deadline Pressure			*
Flexible Schedule		*	
Job Stress			*

Marketing Management Consulting

Management consultants make it possible for companies and organizations to get top talent on a temporary basis while keeping their costs down. You can also market yourself by networking extensively with executives and companies in your area and by building your own website describing your talents and offering testimonials about 'the quality of your work. The key benefits you offer clients are providing a higher skill level than they can afford to get by hiring a full-time employee.

Your Encore Inc. was created to sign up thousands of retirees interested in working on short-term projects, with a focus on research and development. The company's motto is the catchy phrase "People don't retire anymore; they just go on to do other things." But you don't need to go through an agency to get work in this field. You can contact them at (317) 226-9301 or go to www.yourencore.com. The following list will give you some ideas

127

on how to develop a marketing and sales base for a management consulting business:

- Register on employment sites like *thephoenixlink.com* and others that represent high-level executives seeking temporary contract work.

- Join business groups such as the chamber of commerce in order to develop relationships with executives in your community to let them know about your skills and availability. In many major cities you can also find interim executive networking groups.

- Teach courses at community colleges that might attract startup business owners and entrepreneurs.

- Offer to sit in on one or two meetings with a potential client to provide advice for free. You may end up proposing ideas they like but need you to handle.

- Create a website that identifies what services you offer so that potential customers using a search engine will find your site.

What to Charge

Interim executives typically charge on a project-by-project basis, or they use a daily or monthly rate, depending on the assignment. They can typically obtain fees that are higher than their previous salary, especially if they are not receiving other employment benefits and are treated as an independent contractor. Fees generally exceed $100 an hour and $250 an hour fees are common.

Financial Projections

Apply the information in the following financial projection table will help you setup your own financial projections in the templates covered in the Appendix.

Management Consulting Business Financial Projections	
Funding Requirements	Projecting what you will expend starting up this business should be minimal if you already have the computer equipment you need. If not, include those costs in your funding requirements worksheet.
Income and Expenses	Projected total monthly revenue is subtracted from total monthly expenses to determine it you broke even or made money to make on a per hour basis.
Cash Flow	Source of cash usually come from service sales. Your use of cash to meet expenses is deducted to determine remaining cash, which is the total source of cash for each month.
Assets and Liabilities	The balance sheet lists your assets and liabilities, allowing you to determine what your net worth or equity position is in the business. Assets are items that your business owns that have a cash value. Liabilities are debts that your business owes. Your net worth is the difference between the two.

Putting It All Together

The information sources in the table below will help you develop and finalize your business plan for a management consultant business. Sources for additional information are summarized as follows:

Associations

Association of Management Consultants; (212) 262-3055 www.amcf.com

Books & Publications

Million Dollar Consulting by Alan Weiss and his other books include *Getting Started in Consulting* and *How to Establish a Unique Brand in the Consulting Profession, The Consultant's Toolkit: High-Impact Questionnaires, Activities* and *How-to Guides for Diagnosing and Solving Client Problems*

How *to Become a Successful Consultant in Your Own Field* by Hubert Bermont (Crown, 1997)

High-Impact Consulting by Robert H. Schaffer (Jossey-Bass, 2002)

Consulting for Dummies by Bob Nelson and Peter Economy (For Dummies, 1997)

Websites

Consulting Central at consultingcentral.com

The Phoenix Link: (972) 612-8425; *thephoenixlink.com*

Resources Connection: (714) 430-6400, *resourcesconnection.com*

Your Encore, Inc.: (317) 226-9301; *www.yourencore.com*

Market Consulting

Marketing is an essential skill that every business needs, regardless of its size. If you have a solid background in sales and marketing, your consulting opportunities are numerous. Top-notch marketing consultants are in high demand and many specialize in one particular marketing discipline, while the more experienced consultants handle the full range of marketing activities for their clients. You can secure business by promoting the service at networking meetings, initiating a direct-mail advertising campaign, through a well-promoted website, or working the telephone and setting appointments with business professionals to present the benefits of your services. Marketing consultants with proven results are earning $100 or more an hour. Home business requirements include little more than a fast computer, communication tools, and shelves for the latest marketing books and magazines. Use the information and ideas in the following sections to create a market consulting business plan.

Business Overview

Market consultants can specialize in several specialty areas. The Institute of Management Consulting recognizes 30 types of marketing consultants in related areas such as product development and public relations. Most marketing consultants are more than brains-for-hire. Increasingly marketing consultants are called upon to implement what they recommend. That's where their experience comes in and allows them to respond to every prospective client's universal concern. Does this person really know what they're doing? So think of experience as a track record in using one's expertise to solve problems and in the process add value to a client's organization. Because of an increased emphasis on bottom-line results, adding value has become the measure of experience.

Market Consulting Overview			
	Low	Medium	High
Cost to Start		*	
Operating Costs		*	
Potential Earnings			*
Computer Skills		*	
Deadline Pressure			*
Flexible Schedule		*	
Job Stress		*	

Marketing Market Consulting

If you've worked for one organization doing much the same thing over a long period of time, making yourself marketable as a consultant may mean volunteering to non-profit organizations in order to add breadth to your track record. In addition to expertise and experience, every consultant must have first-rate communication and people skills to understand the human aspects that are part of every organizational. Consultants also need to be able to write clearly and present themselves and their findings to senior executives and managers. These skills are equally important in providing consulting to individuals.

Because referrals and repeat business are going to be the most important sources of new business, you will need to consistently and continually nurture repeat and referral business. This means finding gateways into the awareness of key contacts. Having a regular newsletter may accomplish this with some, but get filtered out by others. With the wholesale transition of most communication to e-mail, faxes and telephone calls get noticed when just a few years ago they wouldn't have.

Networking in organizations and group meetings works great. Consider participating in two types of organizations: (1) those whose memberships include potential clients and referral sources, such as industry and trade groups; (2) those such as professional associations, whose memberships include people in your own field with whom you may collaborate with in various ways-mutual-referral arrangements, cross-promotions, joint ventures, independent alliances, satellite subcontracting, consortiums, partnerships, and virtual organizations. The following list will give you some ideas on how to develop a marketing and sales base for a market consulting business:

- If you're willing to bid your services at prices less than what you would charge a local client, check out websites like *elance.com guru com,* and *expertmarketplace.com* where buyers seeking services look for providers to bid on their projects.

- If you have a research and writing bent, "informational inquiries" can give you an opportunity to learn about a company or organization and form a relationship within the organization. Arrange for an interview with prospective clients for an article you will write on a subject of interest to them and your field.

- Obtaining referrals and doing overload work for CPA firms, accounting firms, and financial planners. Get listed as a support service in referral services that professional associations maintain for their members.

- Create a website that identifies what services you offer so that potential customers using a search engine can find your site. Web directories like *switchboard.com* and *anywho.com.* Consider placing ads on local directory sites like *Yahoo Get Local* and *SuperPages.*

What to Charge

Consultants usually bill either by the hour or the project. Hourly rates vary with the type of client, your field, and, of course, location. For small businesses and highly competitive fields, billing $75 to $150 an hour is common. For larger companies or specialties that are in high demand, expect to bill $150 and more. Experienced consultants are able to safely estimate the number of hours a project will require and can quote a project price, which is usually preferred over hourly rates by smaller businesses.

Financial Projections

Apply the information in the following financial projection table will help you setup your own financial projections in the templates covered in the Appendix.

Market Consulting Business Financial Projections	
Funding Requirements	Projecting what you will expend starting up this business should be minimal if you already have the computer equipment you need. If not, include those costs in your funding requirements worksheet.
Income and Expenses	Projected total monthly revenue is subtracted from total monthly expenses to determine it you broke even or made money to make on a per hour basis.
Cash Flow	The cash flow projection shows how money will flow into your business in the form of revenues and flow out of the business in the form of expenses.
Assets and Liabilities	The balance sheet lists your assets and liabilities, allowing you to determine what your net worth or equity position is in the business. Assets are items that your business owns that have a cash value. Liabilities are debts that your business owes. Your net worth is the difference between the two.

Putting It All Together

The information sources in the table below will help you develop and finalize your business plan for a market consulting business. Sources for additional information are summarized as follows:

Associations

The Institute of Electrical and Electronics Engineers (IEEE) Consultants' Services: *www.ieeeusa.org*

Institute of Management Consultants (IMC): (800) 221-2557 *www.imcusa.org*

Books & Publications

Million Dollar Consulting by Alan Weiss and his other books include *Getting Started in Consulting, How to Establish a Unique Brand in the Consulting Profession, The Consultant's Toolkit: High-Impact Questionnaires, Activities and How-to Guides for Diagnosing and Solving Client Problems*

How to Become a Successful Consultant in Your Own Field by Hubert Bermont (Crown, 1997)

High-Impact Consulting by Robert H. Schaffer (Jossey-Bass, 2002)

Consulting for Dummies by Bob Nelson and Peter Economy (For Dummies, 1997)

Websites

Consulting Central at consultingcentral.com

Office Support

Office support specialists is a catch-all phrase for a wide variety of contracted work, including word processing, transcription, editing and proofreading, business writing, preparing spreadsheets or databases, maintaining contact management programs, bookkeeping, billing, notary services, desktop publishing, graphic design, multimedia presentations, office management and organization consultation, answering services, mailing preparation, resume writing to name a few.

Office support specialists typically market to a variety of clients. One of the larger markets includes new businesses and small businesses that do not have full-time office support staffs. Your clients could be business managers, real estate and insurance agents, doctors, attorneys, or any small business where the proprietor has little time to do their own administrative work. Use the information and ideas in the following sections to create an office support business plan.

Business Overview

Administrative and executive assistant, office manager, information processor, and other administrative staff experience provide an excellent background to startup an office support business. Since people are expecting you to create documents they can't prepare themselves, you need above average knowledge and familiarity with various software packages from word processing and desktop publishing to graphic design, database, spreadsheet, and presentation software. Your background should reflect your dedication to details and meeting deadlines. Since a good portion of this business involves working closely with people, it also helps to be reassuring, confident, and punctual.

Office Support Overview			
	Low	**Medium**	**High**
Cost to Start	*		
Operating Costs		*	
Potential Earnings	*		
Computer Skills			*
Deadline Pressure		*	
Flexible Schedule		*	
Job Stress		*	

Marketing Office Support

Competition in the office support field can be stiff, but tailoring your business to a few specific markets is one way to carve out a niche for yourself. You can specialize in one or several of these areas or you can become a jack-of-all-trades, depending on your skills, interests, and what the needs are in the area in which you live. Some specialties, such as database work or transcribing legal and medical materials, pay better than others but require more specialized training.

Find out how other office support services in your market area are specializing with an eye to determine if there is an unmet market you can go after. As businesses and individuals increasingly incorporate technology into their businesses, success in office support becomes more dependent on specializing in doing things that clients' need. Get certified in the Microsoft Office Suite (microsoft.com/traincert) to add credibility to your skills. Name your business to appeal to your market. Pick a name that clearly connotes what you specialize in. Offer discounts on future work to clients and others who refer clients to you. The following list will give you some ideas on how to develop a marketing and sales base for an office support business:

- Contact sales reps and traveling executives who need office support while they are on the road.

- Publishing firms need all kinds of support formatting and editing of their manuscripts.

- Participate in one or more business networking groups or referral organizations for customer prospects.

- Create a website. Because your business is local, be sure to use the name of the community or communities you serve on your home page, in key words, and if possible in your domain name. List your services and provide copies of testimonial letters.

- List your business in the Yellow Pages. Test listing under multiple categories such as Secretarial Services, Word Processing, Desktop Publishing, and Resume Service.

- Advertise in newspapers and church, club, and chamber of commerce bulletins.

- Approaching office business centers about offering your services to their clients.

- Contact with other office support firms about doing overload or work you specialize in that they do not. You can set up reciprocal referral agreements where you send them the kind of work you don't do and vice versa.

- Network inside business and trade organizations such as the chamber of commerce and business referral organizations.

- Have a website that identifies what services you offer so that potential customers using a search engine will find your site.

- Call on firms within your market area and introduce yourself and your business.

What to Charge

Hourly rates range from a low of about $20 an hour to $50 an hour. Services such as desktop publishing, graphic design, database and spreadsheet work, or writing and editing bear higher hourly rates, as much as $75 per hour. Before setting your rate, find out what other secretarial services located within your market area are charging.

Rates for simple manuscript typing are generally less. The key to success in this business is to ensure that you are detailed oriented, can work quickly, and produce work of impeccable quality. You must also build a reputation that you are able to meet all deadlines. To be competitive, it helps to offer pickup and delivery (some services charge for this and some don't), though much of your work may be Internet transmitted.

To charge by the job, you can use the *Industry Production Standards* guide for estimating time. (See Books & Publications, Manuals.) This guide enables you to estimate and calculate time and charges for a wide range of services. Don't sell yourself short by undercharging, and be sure to find out if your state requires you to collect sales tax on the work you do.

Financial Projections

Apply the information in the following financial projection table will help you setup your own financial projections in the templates covered in the Appendix.

Office Support Business Financial Projections	
Funding Requirements	Funding requirements should be broken into two categories; current funding and future funding requirements as is shown in the financial projections shown in the Appendix.
Income and	Projected total monthly revenue is

Expenses	subtracted from total monthly expenses to determine it you broke even or made money to make on a per hour basis.
Cash Flow	The cash flow projection is important because it can tell you the times during the year when you can expect a cash surplus and the times in the year when you can expect a cash shortage.
Assets and Liabilities	The purpose of the balance sheet is to paint a picture of what your business is worth at any one moment in time. Not included on the balance sheet are non-tangible assets such as goodwill and contingent liabilities such as future warranty claims.

Putting It All Together

The information sources in the table below will help you develop and finalize your business plan for an office support business. Sources for additional information are summarized as follows:

Associations

International Association of Administrative Professionals (816) 891-6600 *www.iaap-hq.org*

Books & Publications

How to *Start a Home-Based Secretarial Services Business* by Jan Melnik (Globe Press, 1999)

Websites

Microsoft offers an office certification program on its website (microsoft.com/traincert)

Personal Coaching

In a little more than a decade, personal coaching has emerged as a distinct field, attracting baby boomers into the profession. Most baby boomers have acquired years of knowledge on how to play the game of life – how to make the right decisions and avoid making the wrong decisions along the way. Personal coaching has evolved into a lucrative startup business where boomers are offering their experience for a fee to coach individual clients. If you like to work with people in a coaching and consulting environment, then here are some of the opportunities that you may want to explore. Use the information and ideas in the following sections to create a personal coaching business plan

Business Overview

Coaches typically work one-on-one with their clients, usually over the telephone. You can design your practice around your life and not the other way around. Coaches specialize by types of problems, by industry, and by outcome. They broadly fall into two categories: business and personal. Personal coaches focus on career transitions, creativity, quality of life, health, and wellness, professional development, relationships, finances, balancing work with life, to name some of the common specialties. You need strong interpersonal skills, particularly the abilities to:

- Form a positive relationship with clients where you can provide support through change and growth.

- Distinguish what clients mean, which is often different from what they say by asking the kinds of questions that provoke clients to expand and clarify their thinking.

- Confront client difficulties without being judgmental and helping them with strategizing, prioritizing, and setting goals.

Business coaches may work with specific types or sizes of companies and may further focus on issues such as business planning, financing, strategic planning, conflict management, team building, partnership relations, and productivity.

Personal Coaching Overview			
	Low	Medium	High
Cost to Start	*		
Operating Costs	*		
Potential Earnings			*
Computer Skills			*
Deadline Pressure		*	
Flexible Schedule		*	
Job Stress		*	

Marketing Personal Coaching

With the changes in family and corporate structure, personal coaching provides something missing in our culture. It provides typical citizens the kind of coaching support star athletes, entertainers, and other performers routinely get. Identify one or more niches or specializations that will help you attract clients. Ones based on your industry experience or extracurricular interests may offer you immediate contacts with potential clients. The best revenue streams are one-to-one coaching by the month, group coaching by the month by way of a corporate contract or groups you assemble, and workshops. The key benefit you offer clients is providing them with a high quality relationship. The following list will give you some ideas on how to develop a marketing and sales base for a personal coaching business:

- Offer free thirty-minute consultations to client prospects.

- Make yourself visible by networking in organizations like women's, entrepreneurial and artists groups where you are likely to meet people wanting to change or grow.

- Have a website that tells your specialization and approach along with client endorsements.

- Get listed in directories like *findacoach.com* and the International Coach Federation's Coach Referral Service.

- Speak before groups, giving workshops and seminars.

- Write articles about coaching for print and electronic publications, such as newsletters. Produce their own publications, including booklets and tapes.

- The best referrals come from your own clients who become your evangelists. Most likely clients are people in some form of transition, typically between the ages of thirty-five and fifty-five.

- Networking face-to-face inside business and trade organizations such as the chamber of commerce and business referral organizations.

- List your business in Web directories like *switchboard.com* and *anywho.com*.

What to Charge

How much should you charge will depend on the geographical area covered by your business? Most independent accountants charge by the hour with fees ranging between $50 and $175 an hour. Some charge below $50, and a few can command more than $175 an hour depending on locale and the industries they work in.

Financial Projections

Apply the information in the following financial projection table will help you setup your own financial projections in the templates covered in the Appendix.

Personal Coaching Business Financial Projections	
Funding Requirements	Funding requirements should be broken into two categories; current funding and future funding requirements as is shown in the financial projections shown in the Appendix.
Income and Expenses	Projected total monthly revenue is subtracted from total monthly expenses to determine if you broke even or made money.
Cash Flow	The cash flow projection shows how money will flow into the business in the form of cash and flow out of the business for paid expenses usually monthly to make on a per hour basis.
Assets and Liabilities	Knowing what your personal financial situation is (i.e., net worth) on a monthly basis important because it will enable you to determine how you business is doing financially over time.

Putting It All Together

The information sources in the table below will help you develop and finalize your business plan for a personal coaching business. Sources for additional information are summarized as follows:

Associations

The International Coach Federation (ICF): (888) 423-3131, *www.coachfederation.org*

Books & Publications

Coaching with Spirit by Teri Belf (Jossey-Bass/Pfeiffer, 2002)

Getting Started in Personal and Executive Coaching by Stephen Fairley and Chris Stout (John Wiley & Sons, 2003)

Leading High Impact Teams: The Coach Approach to Peak Performance by Cynder Niemela and Rachael Lewis (High Impact Pub, 2001)

Personal and Executive Coaching by Jeffrey Auerbach (Executive College Press, 2001)

Websites

See a list comparing the many coaching schools at *www.coachingschools.org*

Coach University, *www.coachu.com* or (800) 48COACH, (604)990-3545

Academy for Coach Training: (800) 897-8707, *www.coachtraining.com*

Pet Caretaking

Taking care of peoples pets has grown into a multi-billion dollar industry. A higher percentage of American households have more pets than children. This includes cats, dogs, fish, birds, reptiles, rabbits, small pigs, plus more exotic creatures. Unlike in the past when animals were work animals or yard dogs, today in most homes they're part of the family. Since it is usually inconvenient to take pets to work or along for most travel, many pet owners are using pet caretakers rather than boarding their beloved animals in a cage. Many animals need extra attention and training. As the pet population continues to grow, so does the amount of money people are spending on grooming and pet care. If you have a love for animals, then this may be a startup that may appeal to you. Use the information and ideas in the following sections to create a pet caretaking business plan.

Business Overview

Most people entering pet-sitting have administrative or management backgrounds or have worked as veterinary technicians or assistants, but anyone with an interest in animals who attends to details, assumes responsibility, and interacts with animals can consider pet-sitting.

Because dogs rely more than any other nonhuman species on the emotional messages conveyed by our tone of voice, posture, and facial expressions, having a way with dogs is the primary qualification. People come from a range of backgrounds including teachers, military personnel involved with canine units, former police officers, and psychotherapists.

If you would like to take animals into your home for "animal day care," you need to find out if there are zoning or homeowner-association restrictions that would stand in your way. Some pet day-care services add to their appeal and revenue by offering additional services, like nail trimming, ear cleaning, wing trims for birds, and obedience training, though you may wish to contract with a specialist to provide these services. Specialization possibilities include particular behavior problems or psychological disorders, particular types of dogs, like hunting dogs who won't hunt.

Pet Caretaking Overview			
	Low	Medium	High
Cost to Start	*		
Operating Costs	*		
Potential Earnings		*	
Computer Skills	*		
Deadline Pressure		*	
Flexible Schedule			*
Job Stress		*	

Marketing Pet Caretaking

Everyone appreciates a well-behaved pet that minds and is well behaved. Pet trainers and behavioral consultants work with pet owners to help them teach their pets how to be better members of the household. While most people just want safe, reliable, consistent care for their pets, some pet owners have quite specific demands for their animals' care, so it's important for you to communicate clearly what services you provide and if you're willing to provide extra levels of services. Negotiate a fee that will cover the additional work. The following list will give you some ideas on how to develop a marketing and sales base for a pet caretaking business:

- Advertise in local papers, offering a discount for first-time customers and place ads on local Web community sites, such as *www.petwalk.comin*.

- List in the Yellow Pages and have incoming calls directed to your cell phone so you can be reached while you're servicing your clients.

- Establish active referral relationships with veterinarians, travel agents, cleaning services, pet groomers, pet food and supply stores, or any place pet owners might ask about finding someone to mind their pets. You can offer reciprocal referral services to them.

- Develop relationships with other pet-sitters so you can back one another up in case of emergencies. This will also lead to referrals when another pet-sitter doesn't have an opening or doesn't want to take on a type of animal.

- Have a website with client endorsements and list your services, fees and approach.

- Get referrals from organizations like Pet Sitters International, through which you can also obtain bonding and liability insurance.

- Conduct classes in a dog park where people can meet you.

- Developing referral relationships with veterinarians. Vets refer behavioral problems to specialists.

- Listing in the Yellow Pages with your calls being forwarded to your cell phone so you can be reached while you're servicing your clients.

What to Charge

Prices vary from region to region, but home visits generally run $15 to $20 for up to three pets. If there are additional animals, if the owner wants pets exercised or walked, and for holiday and after-hour service, a higher price is justified. Two visits a day range from $20 to $35 per day; additional visits, more. Doing household chores or providing other services, like key pickup and return, picking up dry cleaning, collecting mail and newspapers, alternating lighting, or watering plants justify a per-service or hourly charge.

With pricing varying considerably by location, training and consulting on an hourly basis in the home ranges from $30 to $100, with $60 an hour being a popular rate for experienced trainers. Classes range from $30 to $300 for six sessions with $165 a popular price point. Some consultants offer a $125 package consisting of a training plan with a 60- to 90-minute visit.

Financial Projections

Apply the information in the following financial projection table will help you setup your own financial projections in the templates covered in the Appendix.

Pet Caretaking Business Financial Projections	
Funding Requirements	Funding requirements should be broken into two categories; current funding and future funding requirements as is shown in the financial projections shown in the Appendix.
Income and Expenses	Projected total monthly revenue is subtracted from total monthly expenses to determine if you broke even or made money.
Cash Flow	For new start-ups, the cash flow projections are important because it tells you the times in the year when you can expect a cash surplus and the times when you can expect a cash shortage.
Assets and Liabilities	Includes all cash on hand and in bank accounts plus short-term investment that can be converted into cash in less than 30 days, such as certificates of deposits as assets.

Putting It All Together

The information sources in the table below will help you develop and finalize your business plan for a pet caretaking business. Sources for additional information are summarized as follows:

Associations

American Dog Trainers Network at *www.inch.como-dogs*

Association of Companion Animal Behavior Counselors: *www.animalbehaviorcounselors.org*

Association of Pet Dog Training: (800) 738-3647; *www.apdt.com*

National Association of Dog Obedience Instructors, Inc.: *www.nadoi.org*

International Association of Dog Behavior Consultants: *www.iadbc.org*

Books & Publications

Don't Shoot the Dog by Karen Pryor (Bantam, 1999)

So You Want to *Be a Dog Trainer* by Nicole Wilde (Phantom Publishing, 2001)

Websites

Dr. Ian Dunbar Dog Behavior & Training Seminars: (707) 745-4237; *www.puppyworks.com*

DogProblems.com: discussion group and loads of links at *dogproblems.com*

Photography and Video Services

For more than half a century, photography and video has played a part in the lives of most people-from baby pictures to videos of bar mitzvahs and graduations; wedding albums we treasure for a lifetime or fine art to adorn our homes. For important life and business events each year, millions of individuals and companies hire photographers to take the top-quality photos and videos they cannot take. So if you've always had a passion for photography, perhaps it's time to use to your creative spirit to launch your next career. Use the information and ideas in the following sections to create a photography and video services business plan.

Business Overview

You may be wondering how someone can make a living in photography these days after the invention of digital cameras and simple printers that allow anyone to print beautiful color photos. Indeed, many professional photographers were worried that digital cameras would damage their business, but the opposite occurred. Digital photography has also drastically improved the market for many photographers who can now sell their work to anyone anywhere. Digital photography has not changed the skills required to be in the photography business today. You still need a good eye for composition and artistic ability. As a professional photographer, you can be a generalist or you can specialize in areas that are of particular interest to you. For example, if you enjoy interacting with people, you might specialize in:

- Portraits addressing the needs of the more than one in five American households that have professional photographs taken during the course of a year.

- School photos, which include class pictures, and may extend to sports-team photos that you sell to parents and class reunions.

- Wedding and bar mitzvah photographs, which involve lots of contact with clients and their families.

- Product photos taking photographs for advertisements, catalogues, and sales materials.

- If you love animals, you can spend your days capturing the victory poses of people's pets specializing in pet photos.

- Nature photography where you can focus on landscapes, rivers, mountains, sunsets, sunrises, and other natural phenomena and sell you photos to the public.

- Sports photography where you capture the excitement of sports such as hang gliding, skydiving, and auto racing. You market your photos to magazines.

Photography and Video Services Overview			
	Low	Medium	High
Cost to Start		*	
Operating Costs		*	
Potential Earnings			*
Computer Skills		*	
Deadline Pressure			*
Flexible Schedule		*	
Job Stress		*	

Marketing Photography and Video Services

If meeting deadlines for assignments is not to your taste, you can participate in the $800 million-a-year stock photography field. Stock photography is distinguished from assignment photography and other specialized fields like fashion photography in that you take photos of virtually any subject you please and sell them to agencies who resell them to people needing photos for books, promotional materials, documentaries, advertising, and corporate or government publications. Another choice is fine-art photography, in which you emphasize creating a timeless masterpiece of any subject as a piece of art rather than as a personal memento for a client. If you wish to pursue photography as a fine art, you might seek to capture highly charged or emotional human experiences, or you might travel the world photographing the beauty of nature selling your work as salon prints through galleries, exhibits, and art fairs or published in books.

As more and more photo buyers take advantage of searching for their specific photo needs on the Web, individual stock photographers are able to sell directly to the buyer from their own websites, without going through a stock agency, so having a website that represents your art and is listed on the major search engines is now a tool of the trade. The following list will give you some ideas on how to develop a marketing and sales base for a photography and video service business:

- Barter the use of your photographs in exchange for free advertising with publications read by your target market.

- Cold-calling potential clients by telephone or in person. You can literally start with the letter "A" in the Yellow Pages and call right on down the list to "Z."

- Create a large portfolio to show prospective clients. Show either the variety of work you do or the specialization you have mastered.

- Gain publicity by donating prints for benefits, auctions, and prizes in exchange for a list of the attendees and their addresses, which you can use to build a mailing list for your own direct-mail advertising.

- Hand out business cards with your website address where people can see your images and order them.

- List your specialty in the Yellow Pages, which will also enable you to be found on Web directories like *switchboard.com* and *anywho.com.* Consider enhanced ads on local directory sites like *Yahoo Get Local* and *SuperPages.*

- Participate in business-referral organizations, trade or community associations that have potential clients and trade associations such as the Professional Photographers Association of America, which has state organizations and local chapters virtually everywhere.

- Selling your images on your own website or on sites like Photographers' Portfolios at *ww.vsii.com/portfolio/homeportfolio.html,* Portfolios Online at *www.portfolios.com.* and *www.sellphotos.com.*

What to Charge

Commercial photographers and video camera men set the price for their work. For work away from home, hourly, daily, and weekly location rates are used (usually between $50 and $200 per hour). Adding special film and materials costs as separate charges helps with overhead. Since negotiating rates is common, having or developing negotiating skills is important for photographers. Also, photographers are frequently unaware of their overhead, so it's not reflected in their pricing. To determine your prices, we recommend consulting with experienced photographers and using a book like *Pricing Photography* by Michael Heron, which has pricing charts for assignment and stock photography.

Financial Projections

Apply the information in the following financial projection table will help you setup your own financial projections in the templates covered in the Appendix.

Photography and Video Business Financial Projections	
Funding Requirements	Projecting what you will expend starting up your business is a critical component of the startup process.
Income and Expenses	Projected total monthly revenue is subtracted from total monthly expenses to determine it you broke even or made money to make on a per hour basis.
Cash Flow	Knowing what your cash position is enables you to manage your money and it gives you the opportunity to secure working capital funding to avoid running out of cash when you have projected a cash shortage.
Assets and Liabilities	Knowing what your personal financial situation is (i.e., net worth) on a monthly basis important because it will enable you to determine how you business is doing financially over time.

Putting It All Together

The information sources in the table below will help you develop and finalize your business plan for a photography and video service business. Sources for additional information are summarized as follows:

Associations

Advertising Photographers of America: (800) 272-6264; *www.apanational.com*

American Society of Media Photographers: (609) 799-8300; *www.asmp.org*

American Society of Picture Professionals: (703) 299-0219; *www.aspp.comOutdoor*

155

North American Nature Photographers Association: (303) 422-8527; *www.nanpa.org*

Photographic Society of America: *www.psa-photo.org*

Photo Marketing Association International: *www.pmai.org*

Professional Photographers of America: (404) 522-8600; *www.ppa.com*

Books & Publications

The Art of Wedding Photography by Bambi Cantrell and Denis Reggie (Watson-Guptill, 2000)

The Photographer's Guide to Marketing and Self-Promotion by Maria Piscopo (Allworth 2001)

Outdoor Photographer magazine: www.outdoorphotographer.com

Websites

Better Photo's website is *www.betterphoto.com*

Photographers News Network's website is *www.photonews.com*

Pool Maintenance

There are millions of swimming pools and hot tubs in North America, all with one thing in common-they must be cleaned and maintained regularly to work properly. A pool maintenance service can be marketed in all traditional advertising media. Consider distributing fliers or coupons throughout your community offering free pool and hot tub water safety tests. The safety test would simply consist of checking the water for toxins and recommending corrective measures to fix the problem. The purpose of the free water safety test is to gain clients for your service on a monthly basis. Contact Pool and Spa Online (www.poolandspa.com) to learn more the pool cleaning business. Use the information and ideas in the following sections to create a pool maintenance business plan.

Business Overview

Pool maintenance services of all kinds are one of the fastest growing segments of the recreation economy. The number of residential and commercial cleaning services more than doubled over the past five years. Of course, home pools are not the only thing that needs cleaning. Usually people that startup a pool cleaning service choose between home and commercial (i.e., hotels and motels) pool cleaning.

Pool Maintenance Overview			
	Low	**Medium**	**High**
Cost to Start		*	
Operating Costs		*	
Potential Earnings		*	
Computer Skills	*		
Deadline Pressure		*	
Flexible Schedule	*		*
Job Stress	*		

Marketing Pool Maintenance

The key benefit you offer clients is providing them with a service that they do not have the time or equipment to do. The following list will give you some ideas on how to develop a marketing and sales base for a pool maintenance business:

- Directly soliciting new home owners that are moving into your market area

- Have your own Web page with its own domain name with testimonial letters from your clients. Have a website that identifies what services you offer so that potential customers using a search engine will find your site.

- Network face-to-face inside home and garden shows for referrals and customers.

- Do overload pool cleaning work for hotels and motels in your market area.

- Call on retail stores that sell pool related products for referrals in your market area and introduce yourself and your business.

- Call on pool installer firms within your market area and introduce yourself and your business for referrals.

What to Charge

How much should you charge will depend on the geographical area covered by your business? Most pool cleaning services charge a flat weekly or monthly rate to clean and provide routine maintenance for a pool. Their rates are based on an hourly rate ranging between $20 and $50 an hour. Some charge below $25, and a few can command more than $50 an hour depending on locale they work in.

Financial Projections

Apply the information in the following financial projection table will help you setup your own financial projections in the templates covered in the Appendix.

Pool Maintenance Business Financial Projections	
Funding Requirements	How much money is needed to start the business and how will the money be used?
Income and Expenses	Projected total monthly revenue is subtracted from total monthly expenses to determine it you broke even or made money to make on a per hour basis.
Cash Flow	Source of cash usually come from service sales. Your use of cash to meet expenses is deducted to determine remaining cash, which is the total source of cash for each month.
Assets and Liabilities	The total value of physical assets owned by the business including equipment and furnishings are listed in the asset column of the balance sheet. The total sum of money owed to your product and service suppliers for outstanding invoices are recorded under liabilities.

Putting It All Together

The information sources in the table below will help you develop and finalize your business plan for a pool maintenance business. Sources for additional information are summarized as follows:

Associations

American Spa and Pool Professionals, www.asapponline.com

Books & Publications

The Ultimate Guide to Pool Maintenance by Terry Tamminen (McGraw-Hill, 2007)

Websites

Home Pool Essentials' website features pool maintenance and improvement advice, www.HomePoolEssential.org

Private Investigations

Security considerations are growing to be a routine part of everything from building design and employment background checks to preventing pirated goods. Terrorism, personal crime, stolen patents and copyrights, corporate espionage, insurance fraud, and missing persons are all unfortunate realities of the twenty-first century. All these nefarious dealings, however, create a huge need for professional investigators (formerly called private investigators). So if you have an interest in becoming a professional investigator, you can train to work as either a PI in a wide variety of specialties and you don't need to have a law-enforcement background.

Television, movies, and novels typically depict PIs working from downtown offices, but in fact, many of them work from home. Being a professional investigator is not necessarily a dangerous business, as most PIs have given up their guns for a computer, a camera, and a car. This is because a large amount of PI work today involves researching people and events via the Internet, tailing them by car to see what they do and capturing their activities on camera. Use the information and ideas in the following sections to create a private investigations business plan.

Business Overview

Only a few states require PIs to be licensed, and some municipalities in no licensing states require them to register with the city or the police department. Some states also require that anyone doing background checking for a fee become licensed as a professional investigator. Licensing requirements vary but usually involve one to three years' experience in some sort of investigative work, such as law enforcement or claims adjusting. Sometimes this requirement can be met by having worked in a collection agency or having done investigative journalism.

Private Investigations Overview			
	Low	Medium	High
Cost to Start		*	
Operating Costs	*		
Potential Earnings		*	
Computer Skills			*
Deadline Pressure		*	
Flexible Schedule		*	
Job Stress		*	

Marketing Private Investigations

One of the most common areas of PI work is background checking, fueled by the need of corporations to prescreen potential employees. Background checking has become commonplace because nearly one-third of resumes contain falsified information, often with serious-enough misrepresentations to cause a prospective employer to pass on an applicant. Corporations have another motivation for background checks these days: the fact that courts are holding companies negligent or liable in cases where employees have been guilty of wrongdoing or violence in the workplace and the company did not prescreen them adequately enough to identify these tendencies.

Background checking involves three types of possible investigations: 1) personal record checking, including credit and criminal history, driving record, lawsuits, and judgments; 2) reference checking to verify the past employers and references given by applicants; and 3) credentials verification, to verify a person's stated educational background.

Some companies have in-house staff that does background checking, but in order to avoid potentially costly oversights and mistakes many prefer to outsource the work to a professional investigator or consultant who specializes in this work. Background checking is also used by people considering business dealings with another company or individual. Given the vast range of work, PIs are used by corporations, attorneys, accountants, insurance companies, employment agencies, collection agencies, and newspapers. The following list will give you some ideas on how to develop a marketing and sales base for a private investigation business:

- Solicit business directly from trial lawyers, insurance companies, and corporate personnel departments.

- Get yourself listed as a professional investigator in the bar-association directories.

- Participate in trade associations and professional organizations for the type of clientele you are seeking (e.g., industrial, law firms, manufacturing companies, etc.).

- Networking local business and trade organizations such as the chamber of commerce and business referral organizations.

- Get listed as a support service in referral services that professional associations maintain for their members.

- Have a website that identifies what services you offer so that potential customers using a search engine will find your site.

- List your business in the Yellow Pages and your website in Web directories like *switchboard.com* and *anywho.com.*

What to Charge

How much should you charge will depend on the geographical area covered by your business? Most independent accountants charge by the hour with fees ranging between $40 and $200 an hour. Some charge below $40, and a few can command more than $75 an hour depending on locale and the industries they work in.

Financial Projections

Apply the information in the following financial projection table will help you setup your own financial projections in the templates covered in the Appendix.

Private Investigations Business Financial Projections	
Funding Requirements	Funding requirements should be broken into two categories; current funding and future funding requirements as is shown in the financial projections shown in the Appendix.
Income and Expenses	Projected total monthly revenue is subtracted from total monthly expenses to determine it you broke even or made money to make on a per hour basis.
Cash Flow	Source of cash usually come from service sales. Your use of cash to meet expenses is deducted to determine remaining cash, which is the total source of cash for each month.
Assets and Liabilities	The total value of physical assets owned by the business including equipment and furnishings are listed in the asset column of the balance sheet. The total sum of money owed to your product and service suppliers for outstanding invoices are recorded under liabilities.

Putting It All Together

The information sources in the table below will help you develop and finalize your business plan for a private investigations business. Sources for additional information are summarized as follows:

Associations

Association of Certified Fraud Examiners 800-245-3321, www.cfenet.com

National Association of Legal investigators, www.nalionline.com

World Association of Detectives, www.world-detectives.com

Books & Publications

Private Investigation by Bill Copeland (Absolutely Zero Loss Inc., 1997)

Introduction to Security by, Robert J. Fischer and Cion Green (Butterworth-Heinemann, 1998).

The Complete Idiot's Guide to Private Investigating by Steven Kerry Brown (Alpha Books & Publications, 2002)

Security Consulting by Charles A. Sennewald (Butterworth-Heinemann, 1996).

Websites

The University of Phoenix offers online education and degrees in private investigating, www.Phoenix.edu

Property Management

A property management business can be started on a limited budget because it is a relatively straight forward venture. Find residential and commercial landlords who are seeking the services of a property manager, negotiate a service contract and start managing. Property management duties include working with handymen and contractors to make repairs, receiving and answering telephone and email inquiries from tenants and owners, and leasing or renting vacant units. A property management service is ideal for a person with a real estate background. Contact the National Property Management Association (npma.org) for more information. Use the information and ideas in the following sections to create a property management business plan.

Business Overview

The demand for property managers will remain strong, particularly in metro areas that have a high concentration of condominiums and seasonal visitors. You'll need to decide upon the scope of your services you want to specialize in. Some managers offer complete services like maintenance and tenet checking while others stick to the basics of taking tenant phone calls and reporting back to the owner. Points to cover in the company introduction part of your business plan are the identification of the types of property management services you plan to offer. Then, clearly state your company's mission (25 words or less) and identify your key objectives.

Property Management Overview			
	Low	Medium	High
Cost to Start	*		
Operating Costs	*		
Potential Earnings			*
Computer Skills		*	
Deadline Pressure			*
Flexible Schedule		*	
Job Stress		*	

Marketing Property Management

The key benefits you offer clients are providing a higher skill level than they can afford to get by hiring a full-time employee. The following list will give you some ideas on how to develop a marketing and sales base for a property management business:

- Have your own Web page with its own domain name with testimonial letters and any articles you have written. Identify what services you offer so that potential customers using a search engine will find your site.

- Participate in trade associations and professional organizations for the type of clientele you are seeking (industrial, law firms, educational, historic sites, etc.)
.

- Showing your expertise by writing articles and letters to the editors of newspapers and business journals. This can lead to being used as a source by journalists.

- Networking face-to-face inside business and trade organizations such as the chamber of commerce and business referral organizations.

- Call on condominium association presidents within your market area and introduce yourself and your business.

- List your business in the Yellow Pages and your website in Web directories like *switchboard.com* and *anywho.com*. Consider placing ads on local directory sites like *Yahoo Get Local* and *SuperPages*.

- Call on apartment owners within your market area and introduce yourself and your business.

What to Charge

How much should you charge will depend on the geographical area covered by your business? Most property managers charge a fixed fee (weekly or monthly) that's based on an hourly rate between $25 and $75. Some charge below $25, and a few can command more than $75 an hour depending on locale they work in.

Financial Projections

Apply the information in the following financial projection table will help you setup your own financial projections in the templates covered in the Appendix.

Property Management Business Financial Projections	
Funding Requirements	Projecting what you will expend starting up this business should be minimal if you already have the computer equipment you need. If not, include those costs in your funding requirements worksheet.
Income and Expenses	Projected total monthly revenue is subtracted from total monthly expenses to determine it you broke even or made money to make on a per hour basis.
Cash Flow	Cash balance is the more important of the two since it shows your projected cash balance for each month and it should always be above zero.

Assets and Liabilities	The total value of physical assets owned by the business including equipment and furnishings are listed in the asset column of the balance sheet. The total sum of money owed to your product and service suppliers for outstanding invoices, including items such as inventory and utility bills are recorded under liabilities.

Putting It All Together

The information sources in the table below will help you develop and finalize your business plan for a property management business. Sources for additional information are summarized as follows:

Associations

National Property Management Association at www.npma.org

Books & Publications

Property Management Kit For Dummies by Robert Griswold (Wiley Books & Publications, 2008)

Websites

Property management software is available at www.PropertyMgmt.BuyerZone.com

Public Relations

A public relations specialist is responsible for promoting their client in a positive and informative manner. Promotion techniques include creating press kits and releases, organizing media and special event conferences, and networking around the clock on the client's behalf. If you have a background in advertising and have dealt with newspaper and magazine editors, TV producers, reporters and other people in the media, you may want to consider public relations. You can use all of your contacts for this endeavor. Getting started in the business can be difficult since the public relations industry is very competitive. As an entry point, consider starting small until you have mastered the art. Contact the Public Relations Society of America (prsa.org) to learn more about the public relations industry. Use the information and ideas in the following sections to create a public relations business plan

Business Overview

Public relations is an essential skill that every business needs, regardless of its size. If you have a solid background in sales and marketing, your public relation consulting opportunities are numerous. Top-notch public relations specialists are in high demand and many specialize in one particular marketing discipline, while the more experienced specialists handle the full range of public relation activities for their clients.

Home business requirements include little more than a fast computer, communication tools, and shelves for the latest marketing books and magazines. Most public relations specialists are more than brains-for-hire. Increasingly they are called upon to implement what they recommend. That's where their experience comes in and allows them to respond to every prospective client's universal concern. Does this person really know what they're doing? So think of experience as a track record in using one's expertise to solve problems and in the process add value to a client's organization.

Because of an increased emphasis on bottom-line results, adding value has become the measure of experience.

Public Relations Overview			
	Low	Medium	High
Cost to Start		*	
Operating Costs		*	
Potential Earnings			*
Computer Skills		*	
Deadline Pressure			*
Flexible Schedule		*	
Job Stress		*	

Marketing Public Relations

If you've worked for one organization doing much the same thing over a long period of time, making yourself marketable as a public relations specialists may mean volunteering to non-profit organizations in order to add breadth to your track record. In addition to expertise and experience, every consultant must have first-rate communication and people skills to understand the human aspects that are part of every organizational problem. Consultants also need to be able to write clearly and present themselves and their findings to senior executives and managers. These skills are equally important in providing consulting to individuals.

Because referrals and repeat business are going to be the most important sources of new business, you will need to consistently and continually nurture repeat and referral business. This means finding gateways into the awareness of key contacts. Having a regular newsletter may accomplish this with some, but get filtered out by others. With the wholesale transition of most communication to e-mail, faxes and telephone calls get noticed when just a few years ago they wouldn't have. The following list will give you some ideas on how to develop a marketing and sales base for a public relations business:

- You can secure business by promoting the service at networking meetings, initiating a direct-mail advertising campaign, through a well-promoted website, or working the telephone and setting appointments with business professionals to present the benefits of your services.

- If you're willing to bid your services at prices less than what you would charge a local client, check out websites like *elance.com guru com,* and *expertmarketplace.com* where buyers seeking services look for providers to bid on their projects.

- If you have a research and writing bent, "informational inquiries" can give you an opportunity to learn about a company or organization and form a relationship within the organization. Arrange for an interview with prospective clients for an article you will write on a subject of interest to them and your field.

- Obtaining referrals and doing overload work for CPA firms, accounting firms, and financial planners. Get listed as a support service in referral services that professional associations maintain for their members.

- Create a website that identifies what services you offer so that potential customers using a search engine can find your site. Web directories like *switchboard.com* and *anywho.com.* Consider placing ads on local directory sites like *Yahoo Get Local* and *SuperPages.*

What to Charge

Public relations specialists usually bill either by the hour or the project. Hourly rates vary with the type of client, your field, and, of course, location. For small businesses and highly competitive fields, billing $75 to $150 an hour is common. For larger companies or specialties that are in high demand, expect to bill $150 and more. Experienced consultants are able to safely estimate the number of hours a project will require and can quote a project at a fixed price, which is usually preferred over hourly rates by smaller businesses. Public relations specialists with proven results are earning $100 or more an hour.

Financial Projections

Apply the information in the following financial projection table will help you setup your own financial projections in the templates covered in the Appendix.

Public Relations Business Financial Projections	
Funding Requirements	Funding requirements should be broken into two categories; current funding and future funding requirements as is shown in the financial projections shown in the Appendix.
Income and Expenses	Projected total monthly revenue is subtracted from total monthly expenses to determine it you broke even or made money to make on a per hour basis.
Cash Flow	The cash flow projection shows how money will flow into your business in the form of revenues and flow out of the business in the form of expenses.
Assets and Liabilities	The total of loans owed by the business to banks and investors will probably be your major liabilities in this business. Once you have determined your net worth by subtracting total liabilities from total assets, you will be in a better position to identify the best financial transition into your new business.

Putting It All Together

The information sources in the table below will help you develop and finalize your business plan for a public relations business. Sources for additional information are summarized as follows:

Associations

Public Relations Society of America: www.PRSA.org

Books & Publications

How to Thrive in the Public Relations Business by Robert Karnecki (Perfect Paperback, 2007)

Websites

Public relation press releases are featured at www.Prweb.com

Real Estate

If you have a background in sales or marketing and like to work with individuals interested in purchasing real estate, then this is a startup area that you may want to consider. Although the overall real estate market was devastated by the recession, there are several unique opportunities for you to consider. For example, retirement communities are one of the fastest growing segments of the real estate market catering to the baby boomers entering into retirement. There are several potentially lucrative options that are available to you if you are interested in investing your time in this profession. Use the information and ideas in the following sections to create a business plan for real estate.

Business Overview

Starting up a business that specializes in residential real estate can take a lot of time and patience, both of which you may not have. In this chapter, we address quick startup ideas that will help you make money in the residential real estate market.

Real Estate Overview			
	Low	Medium	High
Cost to Start			*
Operating Costs		*	
Potential Earnings			*
Computer Skills			*
Deadline Pressure			*
Flexible Schedule		*	
Job Stress		*	

Marketing Real Estate

Apartment buildings are relatively cheap in this post-recession real estate market. They are one of the fastest growing segments of the market catering to the baby boomers who would rather rent than own a home when they retire. There are several potentially lucrative options that are available to you if you are interested in investing your time and/or money in this market. The following list will give you some ideas on how to develop a marketing and sales base for a real estate business:

- Solicit businesses in condominium complexes where you can establish yourself as knowledgeable in knowing the market for that particular condominium.

- Leave fliers and door hangers on homes in areas that you are interested in selling.

- Advertise in local shopper papers and post fliers, cards, and brochures on community bulletin boards.

- Have attractive signage on your vehicle with your phone number and website visible.

- Offer short courses on fixing up a home for sale through local adult-education programs.

- If you live in or near a resort area where people have second homes, solicit absent owners for their business should they decide to sell their property.

- Call on home furnishing stores in your market area and introduce yourself and your business.

- Have your own Web page with its own domain name with testimonial letters and any articles you have written. Have a website that identifies what types of real estate you sell so that potential customers using a search engine will find your site.

- Show your expertise by writing articles and letters to the editors of newspapers and business journals. This can lead to being used as a source by journalists.

- Network inside business and trade organizations such as the chamber of commerce and business referral organizations.

- List your business in the Yellow Pages and your website in Web directories like *switchboard.com* and *anywho.com.* Consider placing ads on local directory sites like *Yahoo Get Local* and *SuperPages.*

What to Charge

Most real estate agents are paid on a commission, based upon the sales price of the property they sell. The standard commission for residential property is six percent and ten percent or higher for commercial property and land sales.

Financial Projections

Apply the information in the following financial projection table will help you setup your own financial projections in the templates covered in the Appendix.

Real Estate Business Financial Projections	
Funding Requirements	Funding requirements should be broken into two categories; current funding and future funding requirements as is shown in the financial projections shown in the Appendix.
Income and Expenses	Projected total monthly revenue is subtracted from total monthly expenses to determine if you broke even or made money.

Cash Flow	For new start-ups, the cash flow projections are important because it tells you the times in the year when you can expect a cash surplus and the times when you can expect a cash shortage.
Assets and Liabilities	First, looking at your personal net worth, are you in a financial position to start the business? If you are not financially in a position to start a new business, you must identify how to raise the money needed.

Putting It All Together

The information sources in the table below will help you develop and finalize your business plan for a real estate business. Sources for additional information are summarized as follows:

Associations

National Association of Realtors, www.realtors.org

Books & Publications

The Millionaire Real Estate Agent by Gary Keller (McGraw-Hill, 2004)

Websites

This website features online real estate schools, wwww.elicenseschool.com

Research Services

If you like surfing the web, you may want to start an internet research service. It's relatively easy to conduct research on the web if you know what you're looking for and how to find it. If you're good at it, you'll be hired by businesses, writers, media editors, professionals and anyone else who needs information but does not have the time to look for it. Billing rates for the services vary, depending on how much research time is required to compile the data. Contact the Association of Internet Researchers (aoir.org) to learn more about this industry. Use the information and ideas in the following sections to create a business plan for research services.

Business Overview

Often you can draw on your experience in whatever field where you've been working. Having had a career in a specialized technical field, for example, might help in developing a specialty in product development research. First-rate computer skills are vital, as are creativity and intuition when it comes to knowing how to develop leads for a case.

Research Services Overview			
	Low	Medium	High
Cost to Start	*		
Operating Costs		*	
Potential Earnings		*	
Computer Skills			*
Deadline Pressure		*	
Flexible Schedule		*	
Job Stress	*		

Marketing Research Services

The key benefits you offer clients are providing a higher skill level than they can afford to get by hiring a full-time employee. The following list will give you some ideas on how to develop a marketing and sales base for a research service business:

- Directly solicit trial lawyers and their office managers, insurance companies, and corporate personnel departments

- Have a booth at conventions of industries you know about or wish to work in where you will meet potential corporate clients.

- Have your own Web page with its own domain name with testimonial letters and any articles you have written. Have a website that identifies what services you offer so that potential customers using a search engine will find your site. Have a website that identifies what services you offer so that potential customers using a search engine will find your site.

- Participate in trade associations and professional organizations for the type of clientele you are seeking (industrial, law firms, educational, historic sites, etc.)

- Show your expertise by writing articles and letters to the editors of newspapers and business journals. This can lead to being used as a source by journalists.

- Networking face-to-face inside business and trade organizations such as the chamber of commerce and business referral organizations.

- Obtaining referrals and do overload work for CPA firms, accounting firms, and financial planners. Get listed as a support service in referral services that professional associations maintain for their members.

- Call on retail stores and service firms within your market area and introduce yourself and your business.

- List your business in the Yellow Pages and your website in Web directories like *switchboard.com* and *anywho.com*. Consider placing ads on local directory sites like *Yahoo Get Local* and *SuperPages*.

- Get listed as a support service in referral services that professional associations maintain for their members.

What to Charge

How much should you charge will depend on the geographical area covered by your business? Most independent accountants charge by the hour with fees ranging between $25 and $75 an hour. Some charge below $25, and a few can command more than $75 an hour depending on locale and the industries they work in.

Financial Projections

Apply the information in the following financial projection table will help you setup your own financial projections in the templates covered in the Appendix.

Research Services Business Financial Projections	
Funding Requirements	Funding requirements should be broken into two categories; current funding and future funding requirements as is shown in the financial projections shown in the Appendix.
Income and Expenses	Projected total monthly revenue is subtracted from total monthly expenses to determine it you broke even or made money to make on a per hour basis.
Cash Flow	Knowing what your cash position is enables you to manage your money and it gives you the opportunity to secure working capital funding to avoid running

	out of cash when you have projected a cash shortage.
Assets and Liabilities	Knowing what your personal financial situation is (i.e., net worth) on a monthly basis important because it will enable you to determine how you business is doing financially over time.

Putting It All Together

The information sources in the table below will help you develop and finalize your business plan for a research service business. Sources for additional information are summarized as follows:

Associations

Qualitative Research Association's website is www.qrca.org

Books & Publications

Successful Business Research by Rhonda Abrams (The Print Shop, 2006)

Websites

Qualitative and quantitative research methods are covered at this website (www.bus.wisc.edu)

Research associate jobs are featured at indeed.com/research-associates

Security Services

Security services are marketed to a variety of business clients needs. Security considerations are growing to be a routine part of everything from building design and employment background checks to preventing pirated goods. Terrorism, personal crime, stolen patents and copyrights, corporate espionage, counterfeit goods, and insurance fraud are all unfortunate realities of the twenty-first century. All these nefarious dealings, however, has created a huge demand for professional investigators and security consultants. So if you have an interest in the security professions, there is a wide variety of contractual work, including overall site security evaluations, electronic surveillance recommendations, and key business operations security. Use the information and ideas in the following sections to create a security services business plan.

Business Overview

Security consulting involves working for clients, who want to protect their employees, property, client lists, or proprietary technology. There are several subspecialties, such as site consulting and evaluating the physical design of buildings and spaces. They're involved in specifying security needs at the design phase of construction and remodeling projects. This may also involve developing electronic security tools for use at the location. Technical security consulting involves specifying, selecting, and installing specific security technologies and products. In forensic consulting, security consultants serve as an expert witness in trials in which security breaches are an issue, such as can occur with fires, thefts, break-ins, etc.

Security consultants are used by architectural firms, contractors, companies building new buildings, museums, banks, stadiums, city and municipal governments, schools and universities, computer facilities, and many other types of employers. Security consultants need not be licensed, though it helps to be certified.

Security Services Overview			
	Low	Medium	High
Cost to Start		*	
Operating Costs	*		
Potential Earnings		*	
Computer Skills		*	
Deadline Pressure		*	
Flexible Schedule		*	
Job Stress			*

Marketing Security Services

Security consultants offer a wide variety of contractual work, including overall site security evaluations, electronic surveillance recommendations, and key business operations security. Security services are marketed to a variety of business clients. Security considerations are growing to be a routine part of everything from building design and employment background checks to preventing pirated goods. Terrorism, personal crime, stolen patents and copyrights, corporate espionage, counterfeit goods, insurance fraud, and missing persons are all unfortunate realities of the twenty-first century,

All these nefarious dealings, however, create a huge need for professional investigators and security consultants. So if you have an interest in these professions, you'll be welcome. You can train to work as security consultant in a wide variety of specialties, and you don't need to have a law-enforcement background. The following list will give you some ideas on how to develop a marketing and sales base for a security services business:

- Network face-to-face inside business and trade organizations such as the chamber of commerce and business referral organizations.

- Obtain referrals and overload work for CPA firms, accounting firms, and financial planners.

- Get listed as a support service in referral services that professional associations maintain for their members.

- Have a website that identifies what services you offer so that potential customers using a search engine will find your site.

- Call on retail stores and service firms within your market area and introduce yourself and your business.

- List your business in the Yellow Pages and your website in Web directories like *switchboard.com* and *anywho.com*. Consider placing ads on local directory sites like *Yahoo Get Local* and *SuperPages*.

What to Charge

How much should you charge will depend on the geographical area covered by your business? Most security service consultants charge by the hour with fees ranging between $25 and $75 an hour. Some charge below $25, and a few can command more than $75 an hour depending on locale and the industries they work in.

Financial Projections

Apply the information in the following financial projection table will help you setup your own financial projections in the templates covered in the Appendix.

Security Services Business Financial Projections	
Funding Requirements	Projecting what you will expend starting up this business should be minimal if you already have the computer equipment you need. If not, include those costs in your funding requirements worksheet
Income and Expenses	Projected total monthly revenue is subtracted from total monthly expenses to determine if you broke even or made money.
Cash Flow	Source of cash usually come from product and service sales. , use of cash to meet expenses, and remaining cash, which is the total source of cash for each month.
Assets and Liabilities	The balance sheet lists the cash value of your assets and liabilities. Total liabilities are subtracted from the total value of your assets to determine your net worth or equity position in your business.

Putting It All Together

The information sources in the table below will help you develop and finalize your business plan for a security services business. Sources for additional information are summarized as follows:

Associations

National Association of Security Companies, www.nasco.org

Books & Publications

Private Investigation by Bill Copeland (Absolutely Zero Loss Inc., 1997)

Introduction to Security by Robert J. Fischer and Cion Green (Butterworth-Heinemann, 1998).

The Complete Idiot's Guide to Private Investigating by Steven Kerry Brown (Alpha Books & Publications, 2002)

Security Consulting by Charles A. Sennewald (Butterworth-Heinemann, 1996)

Websites

40 security roles are defined at this site – www.informationshield.com

Tax Preparation

The stark reality about the American tax system is that it grows in complexity and becomes more confusing for the average tax payer each year. Each year, there are hundreds of changes to the code that can impact the average citizen's taxes. Add to this complexity the fact that the tax forms themselves are redesigned nearly every year, and the end result is that nearly 60 percent of Americans are now hiring someone to calculate and file their taxes. That translates into millions of people seeking the services of a tax-preparation specialist. Use the information and ideas in the following sections to create a tax preparation business plan.

Business Overview

Many tax preparers have prior careers in banking, the military, and government work where they can build on years of experience dealing with complex rules and financial information. If you enjoy working with numbers and like the challenge of mastering the federal and state tax codes, this profession is open to anyone. Most states don't require you to have a special license to prepare other people's tax returns.

One of the quickest ways to start a tax preparation business is to take tax-preparation classes such as those offered by H&R Block. If you prove to be adept in the course, which lasts approximately eleven weeks, you could qualify for a full- or part-time position with H&R Block.

Although there are many excellent software programs that are now available to do tax returns
more easily, millions of people still prefer a tax preparer. Many people get burned by these software programs, when they discover they paid too much tax because they didn't get the advice of a tax professional. So if you enjoy making sense out of numbers, tax preparation makes a good boomer business.

Tax Preparation Overview			
	Low	Medium	High
Cost to Start	*		
Operating Costs		*	
Potential Earnings			*
Computer Skills			*
Deadline Pressure			*
Flexible Schedule			*
Job Stress		*	

Marketing Tax Preparation

To gain experience, consider working for a tax-preparation company part- or full-time, followed by study for and taking of the enrolled agent examination. Focus on people moving into an area. You can save yourself headaches by choosing your clients carefully. You can often lose money by working with a picky client who excessively scrutinizes your work or is too disorganized. The following list will give you some ideas on how to develop a marketing and sales base for a tax preparation business:

- Advertising with your local "welcoming service" gives you access to new people moving into your area. You can purchase participation with a welcoming service by zip code.

- Conduct seminars or teach tax principles for adult education and organizations.

- Contact CPAs who do not work on taxes for referrals or to do overload work for those who do tax preparation work.

- Encouraging referrals from satisfied clients.

- Face-to-face networking inside business and trade organizations such as the chamber of commerce and business-referral organizations for clients and referrals.

- Send personalized mailings to people or new businesses that have moved into your area.

- Using free advertising such as in your local Recycler and on Craig's list *(www.craiglist.org)* on the Web.

- Obtain referrals and doing overload work for CPA firms, accounting firms, and financial planners.

- Have a website that identifies what services you offer so that potential customers using a search engine will find your site.

What to Charge

Prices are either by the hour or a flat fee per return. For a simple 1040 return, rates range from $75 in low-cost areas of the country to $125 elsewhere. Complex tax returns are usually billed by the hour at rates ranging from $50 to $200 and can total several thousand dollars.

Financial Projections

Apply the information in the following financial projection table will help you setup your own financial projections in the templates covered in the Appendix.

Tax Preparation Business Financial Projections	
Funding Requirements	Projecting what you will expend starting up this business should be minimal if you already have the computer equipment you need. If not, include those costs in your funding requirements worksheet.
Income and Expenses	Projected total monthly revenue is subtracted from total monthly expenses to determine if you broke even or made money.

Cash Flow	Use of cash is money paid out to cover the expenses of the business that are due in a particular month.
Assets and Liabilities	The balance sheet lists the cash value of your assets and liabilities. Total liabilities are subtracted from the total value of your assets to determine your net worth or equity position in your business.

Putting It All Together

The information sources in the table below will help you develop and finalize your business plan for a tax preparation business. Sources for additional information are summarized as follows:

Associations

National Association of Enrolled Agents (NAEA): (301) 212-*9608; www.naea.org*

National Association of Tax Practitioners (800)558-3402, (800) 242-3430; *www.natptax.com*

Books & Publications

How to Start a Successful Home-Based Freelance Bookkeeping and Tax Preparation Business by C. Pinheiro (Pass Key Books & Publications, 2009)

Websites

The H&R Block Income Tax Course: *www.hrhlock.com/taxes*

The Tax Resource Group's access to tax research materials: *www.taxresourcegroup.com*

Tax Information for Tax Professionals, provided by the IRS: *www.irs.gov/taxpros.*

Technical Writing

If you like to write and are good at explaining technical things in writing, you can be paid well as a technical writer. That's because whenever any new product involving technology is introduced, there's usually an immediate need for some type of material to document or explain it. Depending on the item, what you write may be either a design specification document, an instructional aide that explains how to use or assemble it, a marketing piece such as a brochure, a magazine or journal article about the item, or a press release for the media.

The audience for your writing might be buyers of the product, installers or repair people, salespeople, or the press. Many items need more than one type of technical document from the above list. The technical writer's job is to make the information clear and easily understood for the intended audience. For this reason, the writer must have a solid comprehension of the product and sometimes of the entire area, category, or field in which the product fits.

- Hardware or software documentation produced as help users learn about applications they purchase

- Policy manuals for government agencies or employment manuals for businesses that must adhere to approved formats

- Product specifications and how-to instructions published on the Web

- Publicity materials such as press releases that follow specific formats

- Training courses that are produced for the Web or on CD-ROM

Most technical writers, therefore, specialize in some area such as engineering or information technology order to ensure that they can stay on top of the latest technical issues. Many technical areas are so complex today that some writers specialize in very specific subcategories of a field, such as microwave technology or financial software. Use the information and ideas in the following sections to create technical writing business plan

Business Overview

Technology is changing at a faster and faster pace, so to stay up to date in this profession; you must always be ready and willing to learn new things about your field. The technical writer must understand the publishing and design issues for whichever format is required and have the technology and software to produce the document in the manner desired. In many cases, this requires nothing more than standard word-processing software, but in others, you may be asked to produce your document as a Quark, PowerPoint, or Visio file. You therefore need to be able to conceive of your work in the context of its final design and publishing medium, and to write precisely to that specification. Once a technical writer works successfully on a project and learns about the product or item in great detail, he or she often becomes an invaluable resource to the hiring company since they don't want to take the time to train another writer.

Technical writing encompasses a wide variety of writing styles and methods of publication, depending on the document you are hired to create. Although this field is growing, it is also becoming more competitive. One out of four technical writers is self-employed. Get ahead of others by being the first to take the initiative to learn about a new cutting-edge technology. Learn as much as you can about a new field or product area to make yourself invaluable to the companies and media involved.

Technical Writing Overview			
	Low	Medium	High
Cost to Start	*		
Operating Costs		*	
Potential Earnings	*		
Computer Skills			*
Deadline Pressure		*	
Flexible Schedule		*	
Job Stress		*	

Marketing Technical Writing

Your key benefits for clients contracting with you as a technical writer are that they (1) get someone with skill sets they probably wouldn't be able to attract, keep, or otherwise afford; (2) only pay for the time they need; (3) don't pay for fringe benefits or office space, and thus (4) can get the assistance they need for a fraction of the cost of a full-time employee, (5) without the need for supervision, (6) increasing your clients' profitability and accelerating their growth. You may make yourself more valuable to your clients by offering more specialized skills such as writing, editing, marketing, desktop publishing, and website design. One large market for technical writing is in-house policy manuals for businesses. These tend to cover business operations and regulatory issues, so getting into this line of work can be easier. The following list will give you some ideas on how to develop a marketing and sales base for a technical writing business:

- Post your resume on on-line job banks and search them for assignments. Most states and cities have on-line job sites where technical writing may be listed.

- Contact agencies that place temporary technical personnel, including technical writers.

- Solicit work directly from companies you want to write for. Some firms may advertise assignments on their websites, so you should search through sites for companies to contact.

- Look for classified ads for technical writers on sites like *elance.com* and *guru.com* and in newspapers.

- Place ads in the trade publications read by your prospective clients in the fields in which you work.

- Offer to write a column for a specialty trade publication in order to get your name out in the field and build a portfolio of work. Participate in association trade shows.

- Create a website where you place testimonial letters and samples of your work. Bidding for projects on websites like *elance.com* and listing yourself on sites like *freeagent.com* and *guru.com* works well.

What to Charge

The Society for Technical Communications (STC) conducts regular salary surveys of employed technical writers and in 2001 found that the lowest end of the pay scale was $25 per hour for those who obtain work through an employment agency and $30 for sole proprietors, while some writers earn up to $85 per hour. The average hourly rate was $44 to $62 per hour. One of the best revenue streams comes from having several key clients willing to enter into retainer arrangements who need you regularly for ten to twenty hours a month. Consider offering them a daily rate, calculated below your hourly rate.

Financial Projections

Apply the information in the following financial projection table will help you setup your own financial projections in the templates covered in the Appendix.

Technical Writing Business Financial Projections	
Funding Requirements	Projecting what you will expend starting up this business should be minimal if you already have the computer equipment you need. If not, include those costs in your funding requirements worksheet.
Income and Expenses	Projected total monthly revenue is subtracted from total monthly expenses to determine if you broke even or made money.
Cash Flow	Source of cash usually come from product and service sales. The use of cash is money paid out to cover the expenses of the business that are due in a particular month. Cash balance is the more important of the two since it shows your projected cash balance for each month and it should always be above zero.
Assets and Liabilities	The balance sheet lists the cash value of your assets and liabilities. Total liabilities are subtracted from the total value of your assets to determine your net worth or equity position in your business.

Putting It All Together

The information sources in the table below will help you develop and finalize your business plan for a technical writing business. Sources for additional information are summarized as follows:

Associations

American Medical Writers Association: (301) 294-5303 www.amwa.org

Institute for Electrical and Electronics Engineers' Professional Communications Society: *www.ieeepcs.org*

Society for Technical Communication: (703) 522-4114, *www.stc.org*

Books & Publications

Handbook of Technical Writing by Charles T. Brusaw (St. Martin's Press, 1997)

How to Become a Technical Writer by Susan Bilheimer (Optimus Publishing Company, 2002)

The Tech Writer's Survival Guide by Janet Van Wicklen (Facts on File, 2001)

Websites

The United States Department of Agriculture Graduate School offers courses in technical writing and writing skills at locations throughout the U.S. (888) 744-GRAD, (202) 314-3670, (888) 744-4723), (202) 314-3300; *www.grad.usda.gov*

Travel Sales

Many baby boomers love to go places and have the wanderlust bug deeply ingrained in their spirit. Whatever the world political or economic situation, few of us are about to give up traveling, as there are still plenty of parts of the world we want to explore. If you are part of this crowd, consider that it is possible to combine your interest and desire to travel with making money and occasionally getting deeply discounted "familiarization rates" for your own travel or tours and at hotels that want you to talk positively about them. You may also be able to get a tax deduction for travel expenses you personally incur in association with operating your travel business, though to enjoy these benefits, you may be asked to demonstrate that you're serious about making a profit from your travel business. Use the information and ideas in the following sections to create a travel sales business plan

Business Overview

Unfortunately making money in the travel business is more challenging as it used to be. First, the Internet has altered the way people make and buy their travel arrangements, with airline tickets and popular tours now being a commodity. Second, you cannot process and prepare airline tickets from a home office. Finally, the profit margins on many travel packages are so minimal that it's difficult to make much money as a travel agent. Nevertheless, there are several approaches a home-based travel business can pursue to make money at travel.

For example, say you are an expert in watercolor painting, digital filmmaking and editing, karate, or salsa dancing. Or maybe you had a business doing something other people want to learn. Why not put together a week to anywhere in the world that people might enjoy visiting while they learn what you have to teach? You could rent a farmhouse in Ireland, a villa in Italy, or a beach house in the Virgin Islands from which to conduct your classes, giving people time during each day to go exploring on their own.

Or why not teach on ship, taking your group on a cruise while they learn? As with tour packaging, it is up to the participants to book and pay their airfare to your destination, but once there, your tour includes arrangements for their food, accommodations, and the classes you teach. Your fees will need to reflect both the value of what participants will be learning and the fact that you have found the accommodations for your customers and possibly made advance deposits using your own money to get group rates for them.

Travel Sales Overview			
	Low	Medium	High
Cost to Start		*	
Operating Costs		*	
Potential Earnings	*		
Computer Skills			*
Deadline Pressure		*	
Flexible Schedule		*	
Job Stress		*	

Marketing Travel Sales

Despite the fact that the Web is full of free travel information, hundreds of thousands of people still buy travel magazines, newsletters, and books, especially those that cover unusual destinations or that contain tips on unique sightseeing ideas and money-saving tips. You can get into travel writing in any of several ways. Become a tour package specialists. As for a tour, you undertake to organize the entire voyage including lodging and meals. However, educational tours are focused on a topic that you have the ability to teach people about as they travel. Where you go mayor may not be related to your topic. Tour packages put together for specialty niche tours that you require some kind of special expertise you have will help you make it in this part of the travel business.

Another way to get started in the travel business is to write for websites. The key is to search for sites related to your travel interests that need better editing and writing and propose to provide this.

Chances are you'll need to promise to help to attract visitors to the client's site to read your work. The traditional route is to write a query letter to travel magazines about an idea you have for an article along with published samples of your travel writing, and then wait for an assignment.

Whichever approach you take to making money from your passion for travel, all involve marketing and sales skills, whether you are selling the public to take your tour, attend your overseas class, buy your book or newsletter, selling an editor or website owner, or generating traffic for a website, but equally important is the passion and expertise you share with other people. The following list will give you some ideas on how to develop a marketing and sales base for a travel excursions business:

- Creating brochures and fliers that sell your tour or trip and include testimonials from satisfied clients.

- Generate referrals from satisfied clients and offer discounts when one client helps you sign up others.

- Have a creative, fascinating website that describes your tour, course, or travel guide for sale.

- Networking in organizations, including business-referral organizations, to develop a tour business drawing on area residents.

- Speak to organizations with members likely to be interested in your travel specialty.

- List your business in the Yellow Pages and your website in Web directories like *switchboard.com* and *anywho.com*.

What to Charge

People who put together tour packages often receive 18 to 25 percent of the total package price. Alternatively, you can arrange the pricing of a tour so that your travel is free, whereby the participants pay a fee that essentially covers all your expenses. Once you establish a schedule and fees for your private tour, you can advertise it via your own website or print up some brochures to mail out upon request. Although your participants will need to purchase their own airline tickets to and from the starting and ending points of your destination, you can mark up the tour package price of hotels, food, and guide services about 18 percent to 25 percent. Or you can save the cost of a guide by doing this yourself.

Financial Projections

Apply the information in the following financial projection table will help you setup your own financial projections in the templates covered in the Appendix.

Travel Excursions Business Financial Projections	
Funding Requirements	How much money is needed to start the business and how will the money be used?
Income and Expenses	Projected total monthly revenue is subtracted from total monthly expenses to determine if you broke even or made money.
Cash Flow	The cash flow projection shows how money will flow into your business in the form of revenues and flow out of the business in the form of expenses.
Assets and Liabilities	Assets are items that your business owns that have value, liabilities are debts that your business owes. The purpose of the balance sheet is to paint a picture of what your business is worth.

Putting It All Together

The information sources in the table below will help you develop and finalize your business plan for a travel sales business. Sources for additional information are summarized as follows:

Associations

Institute of Certified Travel Agents (ICTA) has a distance learning program and lists schools with weekend programs: (800) 542-4282, (781) 237-0280; *www.icta.com*

National Association of Commissioned Travel Agents (NACTA) for home-based and cruise-oriented agents: (703) 739-6826; *www.nacta.com*

The American Society of Travel Agents, (703) 739-2782. *www.astanet.com*

Books & Publications

Home-Based Travel Agent, Kelly Monaghan (The Intrepid Traveler, 2001)
Start Your Own Specialty Travel and Tour Business, Rob Adams (Entrepreneur Media, 2003)

Travelwriter Marketletter: (208) 988-7672; *www.travelwriterml.com*

Websites

Travelwriters.com, operated by *Marco Polo* magazine

Tutoring

Tutoring is on the rise for multiple reasons. Getting admitted to college is more difficult and children are simply not keeping pace with their assignments due to increasingly difficult courses. Also budget cuts and overcrowded classes are motivating some parents to seek out tutors to ensure that their children are learning what they need so they can get into private schools. In other instances, students are so busy with extracurricular activities, on-line chatting, or simply goofing off that they don't study as much as they should and begin failing their classes. Children with learning disabilities or who are regarded as failing under the No Child Left Behind Act also need help. In these cases, tutoring is subsidized under federal law. Use the information and ideas in the following sections to create a tutoring business plan

Business Overview

As a tutor, you can focus on elementary-, middle-, or high-school children, depending on your preference, though most tutoring is done at the middle- and high-school levels. Your educational background or professional work experience will play a role in determining which area of instruction you are most qualified to tutor in such as reading or writing skills, computer hardware usage or software skills, math, foreign languages, history, or one of the sciences. Consider, too, if you have musical skill or expertise in a sport, you can turn this into a niche for tutoring or teaching practice.

Parents usually want tutors to have at least a B.A. in the field they're tutoring. If you want to tutor children under one of the federal programs, you'll need teaching credentials, or a credential related to learning disorders. You need to get to know the curriculum followed in your local schools and buy the textbooks that are used. While you may sometimes teach your own curriculum, you usually need to coordinate with the specific textbook used in your client's classroom. As you build your tutoring practice, you can operate more like a referral service, combining the tutoring you do yourself with providing referrals for students you can't fit into your schedule or who need tutoring on subjects outside your area of expertise.

Tutoring Overview			
	Low	Medium	High
Cost to Start	*		
Operating Costs	*		
Potential Earnings		*	
Computer Skills		*	
Deadline Pressure	*		
Flexible Schedule		*	
Job Stress	*		

Marketing Tutoring

There is a vast market for tutors because many people simply prefer individual instruction since it allows them to learn at their own pace, without the pressure of peers or authorities. If income is your primary objective, consider preparing high-school students for the tests nearly all college applicants are required to take the PSAT, SATI and II, and ACT. These tests are pivotal in determining which college the child will qualify to attend. An adjunct service to college test preparation tutoring is college admissions counseling, in which you help families research and select the most appropriate colleges for their children to apply to.

Tutoring does not have to focus on children or on academic subjects. You can also earn an income by tutoring adults or by teaching a sport or hobbyist skill, such as tennis, golf, dancing, carpentry, or plumbing. Educational therapy that uses both educational and therapeutic methods is another option. Educational therapists help children with attention deficit disorders, emotional problems, family issues, and learning disabilities that get in the way of learning. They are called learning disability specialists in some areas. Some universities offer Educational Therapy certification programs. The following list will give you some ideas on how to develop a marketing and sales base for a tutoring business:

- Post flyers on bulletin boards throughout your community.

- Write articles for community publications on topics that relate to your subject with your photo and byline, including how to contact you.

- Have a website on which you post testimonial letters from past clients. Be sure to place the name of the community or communities you serve on your home page.

- Teach adult education classes in your local schools from which you might obtain private students who need further assistance from you.

- Call on teachers in the subject areas in which you specialize and communicate that you work with students having difficulty and whose parents are demanding more than the school can provide. Also talk with school office personnel, counselors, and principals, leaving behind an attractive brochure that features your qualifications.

- Get to know psychologists and family counselors who are apt to see in their practices children with learning difficulties.

- Have a website that identifies what services you offer so that potential customers using a search engine will find your site.

Pricing Strategies

Academic tutors charge as little $15 to as much as $125 an hour, with most charging between $25 and $60 an hour. Rates vary with subject, grade of the students, experience, your community, and travel time required. Tutors working in their own homes usually charge less than tutors who go to students' homes. Nonacademic tutors can charge between $25 to $60per hour, depending on the skill or hobby you are teaching.

Financial Projections

Apply the information in the following financial projection table will help you setup your own financial projections in the templates covered in the Appendix.

Tutoring Business Financial Projections	
Funding Requirements	How much money is needed to start the business and how will the money be used?
Income and Expenses	Projected total monthly revenue is subtracted from total monthly expenses to determine it you broke even or made money to make on a per hour basis.
Cash Flow	The cash flow projection is important because it can tell you the times during the year when you can expect a cash surplus and the times in the year when you can expect a cash shortage.
Assets and Liabilities	The balance sheet lists your assets and liabilities, allowing you to determine what your net worth or equity position is in the business. Assets are items that your business owns that have a cash value. Liabilities are debts that your business owes. Your net worth is the difference between the two.

Putting It All Together

The information sources in the table below will help you develop and finalize your business plan for a tutoring business. Sources for additional information are summarized as follows:

Associations

Association of Educational Therapists: (800) 286-4267; *www.aetonline.org*

National Tutoring Association: (866) 311-6630; *www.ntatutor.org*

Books & Publications

Tutoring Matters:, Jerome Rabow and Tiffani Chin (Nima Fahimian, 1999)

Tutoring as a Successful Business, Eileen Kaplan Shapiro (Nateen Publishing, 2001)

How to Start a Home-Based Tutoring Business by Beth Lewis (Globe Pequot Press, 2010)

Websites

A collection of articles about tutoring is available at www.the tutoringbusiness.com. All about the home-based tutoring business, www.hometutoringbusiness.com

Appendix A

Financial Projection Templates

This section displays your wisdom and understanding of your business from a financial perspective. Remember that planning is about making good decisions, applying focus and enforcing priorities, not about testing your knowledge. The financial projection templates that are included in this chapter should make it relatively easy to complete each of the financial projections.

Funding requirements: How much money is needed to start the business and how will the money be used? Funding requirements should be broken into current funding requirements and future funding requirements.

Income statement projection: The income statement projection is used to determine how much you must sell to cover all costs and break even or make a profit. Projected total revenue made over a specific period of time (usually monthly) is subtracted from total monthly expenses to determine if you broke even or made money.

Cash flow projection: The cash flow projection shows how money will flow into your business in the form of revenues and flow out of the business in the form of expenses (disbursements). For startups, the cash flow projection is important because it can tell you the times during the year when you can expect a cash surplus and the times in the year when you can expect a cash shortage.

Balance sheet: The balance sheet lists the cash value of your assets and liabilities. Total liabilities are subtracted from the total value of your assets to determine your net worth or equity position in your business. Assets are items that your business owns that have value, liabilities are debts that your business owes. The purpose of the balance sheet is to paint a picture of what your business is worth.

Funding Requirements

Projecting what you will expend starting up your business is a critical component of the startup process. If you don't have the financial resources to make it happen, then your business plan is nothing more than an academic exercise. How much money is needed to start the business and how will the money be used? Funding requirements should be broken into two categories; current funding and future funding requirements as is shown in the worksheet that follows:

Estimated Start-Up Costs			
Funding Requirements	Amount	Date When Needed	Source of Funds
Current Funding			
Future Funding			

Current funds represent the money you'll need in the first 90 days to start your business. Explain what the funds will be used for, such as purchasing equipment, marketing activities, buying inventory for resale, obtaining business permits, or renovating your home office. Describe any future funding requirements (e.g., money needed 91 or more days out) that you may have. Examples of future funding requirements are business expansion expenses, the addition of a company website, or an expanded advertising program.

Income Statement Projection

The income statement is used to determine how much product or service you sold to either make a profit, break even, or lose money over a specified period of time (usually monthly). It compares total income against total expenses to calculate your profits or losses. Consider expenses for such items such as advertising, auto, insurance, lease payments, taxes, utilities, and any expense that will be borne by the business. Then, on the income side, list all sources of income and be conservative.

You will want to prepare income and expense projections for at least three years and then measure actual performance against your projections at the end of each month of operation. That will enable you to adjust your marketing strategies if actual revenues and expenses do not meet your projected expectations. In a couple of months, you will have a much better idea as to how much you make and spend every month. Use the following figure as a guide:

Projected Monthly Income Statement												
	J	F	M	A	M	J	J	A	S	O	N	D
Sales												
Products												
services												
Cost of Sales												
Gross Margin												
Expense												
Payroll												
Advertising												
Administrative												
Depreciation												
Leased Equip.												
Utilities												
Taxes												
Consultants												
Expense Total												
Profit (Loss)												

Cash Flow Projection

The cash flow projection shows how money will flow into the business in the form of cash and flow out of the business for paid expenses monthly. For new start-ups, the cash flow projections are important because it tells you the times in the year when you can expect a cash surplus and the times when you can expect a cash shortage. Knowing this information enables you to manage your money and it gives you the opportunity to secure working capital funding to avoid running out of cash when you have projected a cash shortage. There are three parts to the cash flow projection:

Source of cash usually come from product and service sales.
Use of cash is money paid out to cover the expenses of the business that are due in a particular month.
Cash balance is the more important of the two since it shows your projected cash balance for each month and it should always be above zero.

Projected Cash Flow			
Account	**Month 1**	**Month 2**	**Month 3**
Sources of Cash			
Cash from Sales			
Cash from Loans			
Other Sources			
Total Cash			
Use of Cash			
Operations			
Payables			
Loan Payments			
Assets			
Taxes			
Utilities			
Taxes			
Consultants			
Cash Used			
Cash Balance			

Balance Sheet

The balance sheet lists your assets and liabilities, allowing you to determine what your net worth or equity position is in the business. Assets are items that your business owns that have a cash value. Liabilities are debts that your business owes. Your net worth is the difference between the two. Not included on the balance sheet are non-tangible assets such as goodwill and contingent liabilities such as future warranty claims. The purpose of the balance sheet is to paint a picture of what your business is worth at any one moment in time. The following figure illustrates the format of a balance sheet:

Monthly Balance Sheet		
Account Category	**Explanation**	**$$ Value**
Current Assets	Includes all cash on hand and in bank accounts plus short-term investments that can be converted into cash in less than 30 days.	
Investments	The sum of all investments, such as a guaranteed investment certificate owned by the business.	
Fixed Assets	The total value of physical assets owned by the business including equipment and furnishings.	
Variable Assets	Completed and invoiced product/service sales owed to the business by customers. The total outstanding value of loans made to anybody or business enterprise. The total value of in-stock inventory.	
Total Value of Assets		
Current Liabilities	The total sum of money owed to your product and service suppliers for outstanding	

	invoices, including items such as inventory and utility bills.	
Short-Term Loans	The total sum of short-term loans due in 60 days or less.	
Long Term	The total principal sum of long-term loans owed by the business to banks and investors.	
	Total Liabilities	
	Net Worth (Total Assets – Total Liabilities)	

Once you have determined your net worth, you will be in a better position to identify the best financial transition into your new business. First, looking at your personal net worth, are you in a financial position to start the business? If so, are you prepared to risk the money you have to start the business? Only you know the answer for sure. If you are not financially in a position to start a new business, you must identify how to raise the money needed. Knowing what your personal financial situation is (i.e., net worth) on a monthly basis is important because it will enable you to determine how your business is doing financially over time.

Appendix B
Glossary of Terms

401(k) plan is a broad label for a variety of employer-sponsored retirement savings incentive programs.

403(b) plan is a retirement plan available to employees of public schools, nonprofit organizations, or the clergy. It is identical to the 401(k), except that employers need not contribute, and they aren't subject to 401(k)'s stringent Employee Retirement Income Security Act (ERISA).

457 deferred-compensation plan sometimes called a deferred-camp plan, this retirement plan defers an employee's pay by the amount contributed, a characteristic shared by 401(k) and SIMPLE plans.

Account aggregator is an online platform that presents data from multiple accounts in a single interface that stores log-in information and simplifies web access to personal financial information.

Accrual method is an accounting method often used by businesses with inventory; with this method, you report income and deduct expenses when the work's done (you've done all the things you have to do to get paid and all the expenses have been incurred).

Active management is an investment management style that presumes that investments guided by a fund manager and informed by industry and economic insight should perform better than other similar investments.

Adjusted gross income (AGI) is the amount of income calculated by adding work income and other income such as investment interest and dividends or alimony. It excludes such things as alimony paid and the cost of health insurance paid by the self-employed.

Administrative fees are the fees that cover the cost of running the plan itself, including expenses such as the cost of preparing annual reports, running required discrimination tests, and supporting the website and customer service department.

Advertising is a means of informing the public about your product or service.

After-tax contributions are contributions to an IRA that is not deductible from a filer's tax obligation.

Age Discrimination in Employment Act was passed in 1967 and prohibits any employer from refusing to hire, discharge, or discriminate in any way based on a person's age.

Alternative minimum tax was created to close loopholes that enabled some super-rich taxpayers to pay unfairly low or even no taxes by resorting to legal tax shelters. Unfortunately, the tax lacks indexes to inflation, making more middle-class families vulnerable to assessment.

Angels are private investors willing to lend money or equity capital in much the same way as venture capitalists, but on a much smaller scale.

Annual expense ratio is the percentage of plan assets that are paid to cover operating, management, and marketing costs.

Annuity is a financial contract. You buy an annuity with the guarantee that the company-usually an insurance company-will provide a series of regular, fixed payments in exchange. Annuities come in a variety of forms.

Asset allocation is an investment recipe for all an individual's accounts, dictating the percentage of a portfolio invested in stocks, bonds, or cash.

Assisted living is a kind of housing that provides a modest amount of assistance, including bathing, dressing, and cooking meals.

Baby boomers are people born in a flourish of family-boosting activity that followed World War II and continued into the 1960s.

Balance sheet is a listing of assets, liabilities, and an owner's investment in a business as of a fixed date, such as the end of a quarter or year.

Basis is the amount you paid for property (called cost basis) or other amount treated as your investment in property. Adjusted basis is basis increased by additions or improvements and decreased by depreciation.

Benchmark is a standard used to compare performance, such as the Standard and Poor's 500 Index.

Blog is a web log that can be a marketing tool to express your political gripes, position you as an expert, and draw interest to your website.

Board and care is a type of assisted living that generally offers group meals and other activities for residents who want to spend time with friends and neighbors.

Bonds are a form of loan. In buying a bond, you're effectively entering into a contract with the issuer of that bond to pay whatever money you invested, plus interest. Bonds come in a variety of forms.

Book value is the real value of a company. It's calculated by totaling all assets and subtracting debt and liabilities.

Broadband service is a technology that allows the Internet connection to your computer to run faster and better.

Brochure ware is a website that functions like a written brochure, listing your product or services, rates, and contact information.

Business opportunity is a non-franchise arrangement in which you buy a concept for a product or service.

Business plan is a written report describing what a business is all about and where the business is heading in the future.

C Corporation is organized under state law and taxed as a separate person, but treated as a regular corporation.

Call provision are bonds that are paid off prior to their prearranged maturity.

Capital gain tax rate is the percentage of investing profits that must be paid in taxes, calculated as a proportion of the profit or capital gain of an investment.

Career average plans are similar to final pay programs, but based on the average of all the years you work for a company. You may get a percentage of your salary for every year you were in the plan. In other cases, you may get an average for all years you were in the plan.

Cash flow cycle time is the time over which inventory is ordered, paid for, sold, and when the money is received.

Cash method is an accounting method often used by service businesses. With this method, you record income when your client pays you and deduct expenses as they come up.

Cash value life insurance is a form of life insurance that builds accompanying cash value. These come in several different forms.

Catastrophic coverage is health insurance with exceedingly high deductibles.

Certificates of Deposit (CDs) is a form of promissory note; the lender effectively promises to pay you a certain interest rate if you let them hold your money for a specified amount of time.

COBRA (Consolidated Omnibus Budget Reconciliation Act) requires companies with 20 or more employees to allow you to stay on your health plan for an additional 18 months after you leave your job.

Cohousing is a semi-communal living arrangement where separate living units are arranged around a "common house."

Compounding is the effect of money earning interest which, in turn, results in a larger sum that earns even more.

Congregate housing is a variant of assisted living, offering both a level of assisted care as well as private living space.

Continuing care retirement communities involves several types of housing and living arrangements, including independent living facilities, assisted living, and nursing homes. Retirees can remain in the same retirement community, with the option to change the level of care they receive as their individual needs mandate it.

Conventional IRA was the first Individual Retirement Account introduced and defers any tax impact until you begin to withdraw money from the account.

Custodian is the institution that holds your IRA. It can be a bank, brokerage house, or similar place.

Certificate of deposit is a bank's promissory note to repay the amount deposited, with interest, at a future date, typically one month to five years away.

Chat rooms are locations on the Internet in which people interact with each other on a particular topic or area of mutual interest.

Cliff vesting is a vesting schedule in which none of an employer's contribution becomes an asset of the employee until the employee reaches a specified work anniversary. At the anniversary date, the employer's full contribution belongs to the employee.

Closely held corporation is a privately owned corporation whose stock is not traded on any public exchange.

Collection agency is a business that performs collection services, including sending reminders to late payers and suing delinquents on your behalf.

Commercial loan is money borrowed from a bank or other financial institution that specializes in business lending.

Compound interest is an investment principal in which interest is paid not only on the principal saved but also on the accumulated interest from prior periods that has not been withdrawn.

Constructive receipt is the date when income is treated as having been received by cash-basis businesses because it's under their control, even if they don't actually have the cash in hand (a check is income when received even though you haven't deposited or cashed it yet).

Contribution is an amount of cash or other assets deposited in a retirement account.

Cost of goods sold is the cost of inventory items such as materials, labor, and packaging.

Debt is borrowed money for financing a business. The borrower is called the debtor; the lender is called the creditor.

Deductible for insurance purposes is the amount of damage or liability that the insurance company won't cover. For taxes, it's the amount of expenses you can subtract against income.

Deep discount broker is an investment house that sells stocks and funds very inexpensively.

Defined benefit program is a pension payout based on your salary and number of years of service.

Defined contribution program is a program in which money is automatically deducted from your salary before you take possession of it. From there, the money is put into an investment vehicle of your choosing, including mutual funds, company stock, and other options.

Depreciation is a deduction of a portion of the cost of a car or other equipment you own over the life of the equipment (the life is set by the IRS) to reflect its true value.

Direct rollover is a process that directly transfers assets from one retirement plan into another.

Disability insurance provides income if you become disabled or temporarily unable to earn a living.

Discount brokers charge less than full-service brokers to execute trades.

Dividends are payments to shareholders authorized by a company's board of directors. They can be in cash or additional shares of the company's stock.

Dollar cost averaging is a savings strategy involving investing the same dollar amount at fixed intervals. If share prices increase, fewer shares are bought or if they decrease, more shares are bought at the different intervals.

Domain name is the address n the Internet where people can find your website.

Dow Jones Industrials is a stock index made up of 30 of the largest publicly held companies traded on the New York Stock Exchange.

Dying intestate is the legal term that refers to lack of a will or trust that provides instructions after someone dies.

ECHO is an acronym for Elder Cottage Housing Opportunities. This is usually a separate, small manufactured home that is added onto the side or backyard of an existing home.

Employee stock ownership plan (ESOP) is a program that allows employees to buy company stock, often with little or no commission.

Employer identification number is the number assigned to a business owner by the IRS after you file IRS Form SS-4. This is used for identification purposes on tax returns, bank accounts, and retirement plans.

Endorsement is a correction or change to an existing insurance policy.

Entrepreneur is someone who organizes and directs a start-up business, assuming the risk in the hope of making a profit.

Equity is the value of your home after subtracting the mortgage balance.

Equity financing a business happens when you bring investors in as part owners of the business.

Escrow is an arrangement in which a third party holds funds; when certain conditions are met, the funds are paid out.

Exchange traded funds (ETFs) are pooled investment accounts that resemble mutual funds in that they hold a basket of many individual investments but are traded directly on the stock exchanges by investors buying and selling their shares like stocks.

Expense ratio takes in all expenses incurred by a fund's operations and expresses them in terms of percentages.

Face value is the principal; the amount of money you invested when you bought a bond. It's also known as par value.

Fair market value is what a willing buyer and willing seller would pay, if neither is being forced to buy or sell and each understands all the facts and circumstances of the deal.

Fee for service is a form of health insurance that lets you choose any doctor or health care provider you like. Generally, the coverage pays 80 percent of any costs you accumulate.
You are obligated to pick up the remaining 20 percent.

Fee-only financial planner is a financial advisor who charges only for his advice, based on the consultation duration or project scope, and who doesn't sell investment products for commission in order to avoid conflict of interest in investment choice recommendations.

FICA (Federal Insurance Contributions Act) are the Social Security and Medicare taxes on wages paid by both the employer and the employee.

Final pay plan is a pension that can offer the biggest payout, as they average your salary over the last several years you're employed at a company.

Financial statement is information about income, expenses, sales figures, and other number-oriented items such as a cash flow statement, balance sheet, or profit and loss statement.

Fixed annuity is a tax deferred financial instrument marketed by insurance companies and brokerage firms that pays a fixed rate of interest that readjusts annually. Fixed Annuities are similar to CDs in that they pay a fixed rate of interest that readjusts on a yearly basis. Annuities are sold by life insurance companies and some brokerage firms.

Flat benefit plan is one of the most simple and straightforward pension payout. You receive a set monthly amount based on how long you worked for a company.

Flexible spending account is a program that allows you to set aside money from your salary tax-free. These funds can then be used to help pay for medical expenses that are not covered by your employer's health plan.

Franchise is a business arrangement that gives you the right to sell a product or service in a particular area. The company selling the concept is the franchisor; you are the franchisee. The right to a large territory is called a master franchise.

Fulfillment companies are in business to take and processes orders for you, including acceptance of payment by credit card. Generally, a fulfillment company charges a flat fee for their services.

Full retirement age is the age at which you can receive your full retirement benefit from Social Security.

Fund family is several different mutual funds that a company maintains and offers to clients. The funds are usually set up for different financial objectives.

Fundamental analysis is a stock analysis involving examination of a company's operating statistics and numbers.

FUTA (Federal Unemployment Tax Act) is the Federal unemployment insurance tax paid by an employer on an employee's wages.

Goodwill is a favorable reputation of a business, which is considered an intangible asset.

Graded vesting is a vesting schedule in which an employer's contribution vests gradually over time, in stages or grades.

Grants are money from government sources or private foundations to start or run a business that matches the goals of the grant maker; grant money doesn't have to be repaid. .

Gross income is income before deductions. For purposes of the home office deduction, gross income means money from business minus expenses that don't relate to the use of the home such as office supplies or the salary of an employee.

Guaranteed investment contracts (GICs) is a contract involving a guaranteed rate of return.

Hobby loss rules are the tax rules that prevent an individual from deducting business expenses that are greater than business income where there's no reasonable expectation of making a profit from the business.

Home equity line of credit is a loan secured by the amount of equity you have in your home.

Home-office deduction is the total of deductions from the business use of a home office, including depreciation on the office or a portion of rent, as well as the portion of utilities and insurance related to the home office.

HTML (Hypertext Markup Language) is the programming language used on computers to create websites.

Independent contractor is a person who contracts to provide work according to his own methods. This person isn't under the control of the person or business for which the work is being performed (not an employee).

Income tax rate is the percentage of one's income that must be paid to local, state, or federal government.

Individual retirement accounts (IRA) are planned accounts that carry a tax advantage intended to encourage savings.

Individual 401(k) is a retirement savings program best suited for someone who works on their own and has no plans to bring on any employees in the future.

Inflation is the effect of rising prices on the value of money to buy goods and services.

Irrevocable trust is a trust that can't be changed in any way during the grantor's lifetime.

Internet is a worldwide collection of computer networks that you can access with a computer, modem, telephone line, and an online service provider or Internet service provider.

Invoice is an itemized list of products you've sold to someone, stating the quantity, price, and terms of sale; a bill for services rendered.

IRA basis is the amount contributed to an IRA that isn't eligible for tax deduction.

IRA trustee fees are costs paid by the investor that can include sales commissions, management fees, and marketing fee.

Joint and several liabilities is a legal rule that makes two or more parties fully responsible for damages, debt repayment, and other legal obligations.

Keogh plan is a tax-deferred retirement plan that lets small business owners and the self-employed save money for retirement.

Lifestyle funds are investment pools that resemble target-date funds in that they are a mix of mutual funds in an asset allocation that the mutual fund company chooses but that cater to risk tolerances.

Limited liability company is a type of business organization formed under state law that gives owners protection from personal liability but treats them as a partnership for tax purposes.

Limited partnership is a partnership in which one or more partners has limited personal liability and can't participate in the day-to-day operations of the business.

Limit orders is a stock purchase system that lets you establish prices at which you wish to buy or sell.

Living will also known as an advanced medical directive is a document that outlines your decisions about any sort of life-sustaining treatment.

Long-term care insurance is insurance you buy to pay for nursing home care and other sorts of long-term, comprehensive care.

Managed care also known as health maintenance organizations, is less expensive than fee for service. However, you have a limited choice of health care providers.

Medicaid is the federal program designed to pay for health care for the poor.

Medicare is the federal medical care program for persons age 65 and up. It is subdivided into four parts, offering different forms of coverage.

Medigap insurance is supplemental insurance to cover any gaps in Medicare coverage.

Marginal tax rate is the rate on the highest bracket a taxpayer's income reached.

Marketing is how people advertise, publicize, or otherwise inform each other of their product or service with the goal of exchanging products or services with each other.

Matching contribution is the employer plan-match option under which an employer promises to match a certain percentage of each employee's contribution up to a specific percentage of their pay.

Medical IRA known as a health savings account is an individual retirement account in which account holders can deposit pretax money to pay for medical expenses.

Modified adjusted gross income known as modified AGI, is the adjusted gross income from an IRA withdrawal by someone age 591/2 or older, disabled or deceased, using the withdrawals to pay

for college or other qualified higher education expenses, or using withdrawals toward
a first-time home purchase.

Money market deposit account is an investment account that often pays lower interest than a CD, but whose assets are accessible anytime without waiting for a future maturity date.

Money market fund is an investment account whose the cash in the account is accessible at anytime.

Monte Carlo calculator is a calculator that generates a measure of the probability that a given investment outcome scenario will result in a financially comfortable retirement based on expected assets, probable lifetime, and economic conditions.

Mutual funds are a combination of individual investments such as stocks, bonds, and cash bundled together into one product.

Net operating losses are business expenses in excess of business income; business losses that can be carried back 2 years and forward 20 years; also called NOLs.

Net unrealized appreciation is the difference in value between the average cost that you paid for stock and its current market value.

Network marketing is direct sales to consumers with distributors getting money from both direct sales and a percentage of the direct sales of other distributors they bring into the network.

Networking is word-of-mouth marketing in which contacts are made to try to drum up business.

Nonretirement accounts are bank or mutual fund accounts that are not held inside IRAs and on which taxes must be paid as accrued.

Overhead is the cost of monthly expenses, including electricity, telephone, insurance, and salaries of employees.

Partnership occurs when two or more people working together in a business with the intention of making a profit.

Passive management is an investment management style that seeks to match the market's performance.

Personal service corporation is subject to special tax rules; corporation engaged in the fields of health, law, accounting, engineering, architecture, actuarial science, performing arts, or consulting that meets certain ownership and service tests.

Plan provider is the company hired by an employer to administer their retirement plan, who often acting as the plan's trustee as well.

Points represent an up-front interest payment to a lender. One point is equivalent to 1 percent of the amount borrowed.

Power of attorney allows someone to make decisions when you're incapable of doing so yourself. Examples include medical and financial power of attorney.

Pretax contribution to a tax deferred retirement amount that a filer is permitted to deduct from their tax obligation.

Price-earnings ratio (PIE) is a popular stock ratio that illustrates how much an investor would be willing to spend in return for $1 in company earnings.

Price/book ratio (PIB) is a ratio that compares a stock's price to what a company is worth.

Price/sales ratio (P/S) is ratio that is calculated by dividing a current stock price by a company's earnings per share.

Primary insurance amount (PIA) is all your Social Security cash benefits, including your monthly benefit as well as benefits for dependents and survivors.

Probate is the legal process that the state must go through should you die with property still in your name.

Prime rate is the interest rate banks charge their preferred customers.

Profit sharing contribution is an employer contribution to their employees' retirement account that is made based on the profits of the company.

Promotion is the act of stimulating an immediate sale with special offers, such as discount coupons.

Publicly held corporations issues stock that is traded on a public exchange such as the New York Stock Exchange.

QUADRO is a divorce-specific transfer between two people's accounts requiring a court order.

Qualified is a term that means a pension program has to adhere to certain governmental guidelines for tax purposes.

Real estate investment trusts (REITs) are funds that invest in property, including shopping centers, apartment buildings, and similar commercial operations.

Rebalancing are adjustments to an asset allocation that correct for different assets having performed differently over time, eventually comprising different portfolio percentages than intended.

Reverse mortgage is a mortgage that lets you tap the accumulated equity in your home. In doing so, your loan balance increases rather than going down.

Revocable trust is a trust that may be changed or eliminated completely.

Rider is an additional clause to an existing contract or insurance policy to cover a special item or event (usually an upgrade to a policy); sometimes referred to as an endorsement.

Risk tolerance is the amount of uncertainty and volatility with which an investor feels comfortable.

Roth 401(k) is an employer-sponsored retirement account in which tax liability accrues upon contribution but whose account earnings and withdrawals are tax-free.

Roth 403(b) is an employer-sponsored retirement account offered to employees of public schools, nonprofit organizations, and the clergy in which tax liability accrues upon contribution but whose account earnings and withdrawals are tax-free.

Roth IRA is a form of individual retirement account in which taxes do not accrue on withdrawn funds, whether earnings or basis.

S Corporation also called a Subchapter S Corporation is organized under state law that elects to have business income taxed to its shareholders.

Safe-harbor 401(k) is an employee-sponsored plan that reduces an employer's effort and cost in running the plan's nondiscrimination tests.

SBA (Small Business Administration) is a federal agency that sponsors loan programs and other assistance to small businesses.

SBICs (Small Business Investment Companies) are privately managed firms licensed by the SBA to make loans to small businesses.

Search engines are websites that enable you to find other pages on the web, just like a library card catalog helps you find books on shelves.

Self-employment tax is Social Security and Medicare taxes paid by self-employed individuals, such as sole proprietors, on their net earnings from the business.

Self-insured is having sufficient assets to make life insurance unnecessary.

SEP plan known as the Simplified Employee Pension plan is a retirement option popular with people who are self-employed and who don't have employees in which 100 percent of the contributions come from the employer.

Shareholders are the owners of a corporation (also called stockholders) whose ownership interest is in the form of stock certificates.

Shares outstanding are the total number of shares owned by an investor.

SIMPLE 401(k) plan is a plan that combines the features of SIMPLE IRAs and regular 401(k) plans, including contribution limits and employer match rules of SIMPLE plans.

SIMPLE IRA is an acronym for Savings Incentive Match Plan. This type of IRA is particularly suited to someone whose self-employment income is relatively modest-$30,000 annually or less.

SIMPLE Plan also known as the Savings Incentive Match Plan for Employees is a common option in companies with 30 or fewer employees but available to companies with up to 100 employees, an IRA account into which both employee and employer can contribute.

Simplified Employee Pensions is retirement plan available to employers and the self-employed. All contributions are tax-deductible.

Single-person 401(k) also called a solo 401(k) and a self-employed 401(k) is a retirement plan that simplifies the administration of a 401(k) enough to make it affordable for single-person companies and very small enterprises.

Sixty-day rollover is a transfer of assets from a 401(k) plan to an individual retirement account during a 60-day period and that assesses a 10 percent early withdrawal penalty unless the rollover is not completed in 60 days.

Social Security formally known as the Federal Old Age, Survivors and Disability Insurance program provides retirement funding and other benefits to participants.

Sole proprietorship is an unincorporated business owned by one person.

Solution providers are companies that provide all-in-one packages for running an online business (usually for a flat monthly fee).

Start-up phase is the period in which a business begins operation, generally the first three months.

Stock is a share of ownership in a company. Stocks come in a variety of types, with different features and objectives.

Stop loss orders is a method of stock buying specifically designed to limit your losses and protect whatever profit you may have earned from a stock.

Summary Plan Description (SPD) is the book of rules that governs your specific 401(k) plan, including when an employee will be eligible to participate and the specifics about how to contribute to the account and how money can be withdrawn.

Surrender value is the amount you receive if you cash out a life insurance policy.

Target date funds are mutual funds whose allocation of assets are tailored to perform best within a time specific event, like your retirement date.
Tax credit is a reduction in income tax on a dollar-for-dollar basis.

Tax deferred is the income gains generated by investments that do not become taxable until the funds are withdrawn from the account.
Tax-deductible is the quality of income or capital gains generated by investments that can reduce tax liability by the amount deposited into a retirement account.

Taxable income is the earning from an individual's job and investments that are taxable each year.
Teaser cards are credit cards with very low interest rates that last only for a limited amount of time.

Technical analysis is a stock analysis on which a company's trading patterns are charted and analyzed.

Term life insurance is the simplest form of life insurance, as it involves no cash value.

Testamentary trust is a trust, created under a last will and testament that becomes effective only after the grantor dies and the will is admitted to probate.

Timing the market means determining at a particular moment in time, which way the market is going – up or down or sideways.

Treasury securities are issued and backed by the federal government. They come in various forms, including securities, notes, savings bonds, and other formats.

Trustee fees are the cost paid by investors in retirement accounts that can include sales commissions, management, and administration fees.

Trusts is a legal vehicle in which one person (known as the trustee) holds property for another person (known as the beneficiary). This trustee can be a person or a trust company. Trusts are useful in distributing the assets of an estate.

Turnkey business is a business that is ready to go into operation, with all materials, processes, and equipment in place to produce a product or service.

Umbrella insurance is an additional form of liability insurance coverage.

Unearned income is income you don't earn. Common examples are pension and annuity payouts, dividends, and interest and proceeds from life insurance.

URL (Uniform Resource Locator) is another name for a web address.

Value averaging is a variant on dollar-cost averaging that takes into account stock price movement.

Variance is a change or alteration of a zoning rule granted specifically for one person.

Venture capitalists are people or companies that invest in businesses (often technology related) with the expectation of realizing big profits in the future.

Virtual workers are people who do jobs from their own locations, such as answering your telephone from their home offices rather than from your office.

Waiting period is the time between the onset of a disability and when benefits begin.

Will is a written document that delineates how you want your property distributed after you die.

Withdrawal is a cash value of an asset redeemed from a retirement account.

Work credits are a system to determine Social Security eligibility. You become formally eligible once you have accumulated 40 "work credits."

Yield is the effective rate of interest that a bond pays to investors.

Appendix C

Useful Information

Annual Reports

Investor Guide (*www.investorguide.com/stocklist.cgi*) provides links to thousands of publicly traded companies.

Best Calls (*www.bestcalls.com*) provides access to companies' quarterly earnings press conferences.

Public Register's Annual Report Service (*www.prars.com*) offers both online and hard copy annual reports.

Thomson Investor Net (*www.thomsoninvest.net*) covers more than 7,000 in-depth company reports that are updated twice a month.

Security Exchange Commission (SEC) is the official government site that hosts all financial reports of the publicly traded companies in the United States. The site is at *www.sec.gov /edgar/searchedgar/webusers.htm*

Bonds

Bonds Online (*www.bondsonline.com*) provides charts and historical data that compare the various bond market sectors.

The Bond Market (*www.bondcan.com*) specializes in investing in Canadian bonds.

The Bond Market Association (*www.bondmarket.com*) is loaded with information about thousands of bonds and their respective trading history.

Brokers

Charles Schwab (*www.schwab.com*)

Fidelity Investments *(www.jidelity.com)*

T. Rowe Price *(www.troweprice.com)*

Vanguard Group *(www.vanguard.com)*

Budgeting

You can view a sample budget at *www.personalbudgeting.com*. A good resource for developing a budget is available at *www.simpleplanning.net*. The following websites contain good budget tools:

www.flexibleretirementplanner.com
www.smartmoney.com
www.money.com
www.personalbudgeting.com
www.simpleplanning.com
www.tdameritrade.com
www.fidelity.com/myplan

Credit Cards and Credit Scores

To find out about credit card options, visit *www.e-wisdom.com*. The website at *www.cardratings.com* offers a variety of resources to help you understand everything related to credit cards. For a fee, you can find out what your score is at *www.myjico.com*. You can check your credit report at all three bureaus at *www .annualcreditreport.com*. The following websites will provide you with additional information about credit cards and credit scores:

www.cardrating.com
www.cardratings.com
www.myfico.com
www.annualcreditreport.com

Debt Reduction

If you need more advice on reducing your debt, try Barnes & Noble's website *www.barnesandnoble.com)* or Amazon's website *(www.amazon.com)* and browse through their debt-related books. The website at *money.cnn.com/tools/debtplanner/debtplannerjsp* will help you project when you will be debt free. If you are interested in learning more about bankruptcy, go to *www.banhruptcvinfo.com.* Qpicken.com offers a Debt Reduction Planner, an excellent tool for about $50. The following websites will provide you with debt reduction information:

www.defeatthedebt.com
www.cgi.money.cnn.com
www.bankrupcyinfo.com
www.smartmoney.com
www.money.com
www.simpleliving.net
www.debetorsanonymous.org
www.clearbankrupcy.com

Discount Brokers

Accutrade *(www.accutrade.com) 800-494-8939*

American Express (*www.americanexpress.com*) 800-658-4677

Morgan Stanley *(www.morganstanley.com) 212-761-4000*
E*Trade *(www.etrade.com) 800-387-2331*

Fidelity *(wwwjidelity.com) 800-544-8666*

Muriel Siebert *(www.msiebert.com) 800-872-0444*

Schwab *(www.schwab.com) 800-435-4000*

Scottrade *(scottrade.com) 800-619-7283*

Wall Street Access *(www.wsaccess.com) 800-925-5782*

TD Ameritrade *(www.tdameritrade.com) 800-669-3900*

Diversified Investing

Legg Mason's website *(www.leggmason.com)* provides an online questionnaire to help you develop a diversification plan.

Frank Russell Company' *(www.russell.com)* features a Comfort Quiz to help you allocate your investments.

Fidelity's Asset Diversification Planner *(www.fidelity.com)* offers diversification advice, a risk questionnaire, and model portfolios.

The Intelligent Asset Allocator *(www.eJficientfrontier.com)* offers comprehensive information on how to build a diversified portfolio.

Education

To learn more about federal financial aid for college and how to apply, visit the U.S. Department of Education's website at *www.ed.gov.*

The American Association of Individual Investors offers advice on funds and portfolio management on their website at *www.aaii.com.*

Bloomberg Personal Finance *(www.bloomberg.com)* offers online training when you click on the Bloomberg University module.

Investing Basics *(www.aaii.com/invbas)* offers feature articles about how to start successful investment programs, pick winning stocks, and evaluate your options.

Investor Guide *(www.investorguide.com)* features more than 1,000 answers to frequently asked questions.

Money 101 provides an interactive investment seminar at *www.money.cnn.com*. Money's *www.eldernet.comlmoney.htm* offers tutorials and advice on investing in stocks, mutual funds, and bonds.

Morningstar's University *(www.morningstar.com)* offers a comprehensive investment education program. The Motley Fools offer an investment seminar on their website at *(www.fool.com)*.

The Mutual Fund Education Alliance is the trade association for no-load funds and offers advice on how to select funds *(www.mfea.com)*.

Vanguard *(www.vanguard.com)* offers online courses that cover the fundamentals of investing in mutual funds.

Estate Planning

If you want to create a basic will on your computer, Quicken offers a software product called Will Maker that is available in computer stores and at *www.nolo.com*. The following websites will provide you with additional estate planning information:

www.quicken.com
www.nolo.com
www.smartmoney.com
www.money.com
www.kinplinger.com
www.smartmoney.com/retirement
www.mpower.com
www.financialengines.com
www.morningstar.com

Financial Calculators

www.kinplinger.com
www.socialsecurity.gov/estimator
www.fincalc.com

www.dinkytown.com
www.calc.xml
www.dinkytown.com
www.riskgrades.com
www.choosetosave.org/calculators
www.schwab.com
www.troweprice.com/ric

Financial and Economic News

The Bureau of Economic Analysis *(www.bea.gov)* calculates economic indicators such as the gross domestic product and other regional, national, and international data, all of which are displayed on their website.

Census Bureau *(www. census.gov)* provides information about industry statistics and general business conditions.

STAT-USA *(www.stat-usa.gov)* is sponsored by the U.S. Department of Commerce and provides financial information about economic indicators, statistics, and economic news.

Financial Planning Organizations

The American Institute of Certified Public Accountants *(www.aicpa.org)*
Personal Financial Planning Division, 1211 Avenue of the Americas, New York, NY 10036, 800-862-4272

The National Association of Personal Financial Advisors *(www. nap/a. org)* 355 W. Dunbee Rd., Suite 200, Buffalo Grove, IL 60089, 800-333-6659

A website that offers a variety of articles on financial planning is at *ww.money.cnn.com.*

Financial Books, Publications and News Sites

The following websites will provide you with additional financial information and news:

www.money.cnn.com
www.cnnmoney.com
www.simpleplanning.com
www.fidelity.com
www.businessweek.com
www.kinplinger.com
www.morningstar.com
www.kiplinger.com
www.Yodlee.com
www.investools.com
www.quicken.com
www.fidelity.com
www.Smartinvestmentbook.com

Financial Tools

The Financial Center *(wwwfinancia!center.com)* has a financial section for retirees. Choose United States and then financial planning. Under this category, choose retirement. Schwab *(www.schwab.com)* helps you develop a financial plan with its online calculators, tools, and advice. Virtual Stock Exchange by Market Watch *(www.virtualstock exchange.com)* is a stock-simulation game that allows you to trade shares just as you would in a real brokerage account.

Government Agencies

The following websites will provide you with additional government agency information:

www.irs.gov
www.irs.gov

www.completetax.com
www.medicare.gov
www.socialsecurity.gov/estimator
www.socialsecurity.gov

Home Based Businesses

U.S. Small Business Administration (800) 827-5722; *sba.gov*
American Home Business Association (866) 396-7773
homebusinessworks.com
Entrepreneur.com is an online small business resource center providing information and advice on products, services and resources.
Familybusinessmagazine.com offers tips, articles and advice about starting and operating a family business.
Home-based-business-opportunities.com features hundreds of home based and small business opportunities listings.
Homebusinessmag.com is an online magazine with information, advice, tools and links for home business owners.
Powerhomebiz.com provides information, advice and tools for home business owners.
Sbomag.com is the Small Business Opportunities Magazine providing readers with the latest small business opportunities news, information and industry resources.

Index Funds

There are literally hundreds of mutual funds that index every segment of the market. Here are two of the better funds to consider: Fidelity Spartan Market Index Fund, which mirrors the Standard & Poor's 500 (S&P 500) index (800-544-8888) T. Rowe Price Equity Index Fund, which mirrors the S&P 500 (800-638-5660).

Industry Trends

ABC News *(www.abcnews.com)* features articles on current industry news and market expert commentary. American Society of Association Executives *(www.asaenet.org)* provides high quality industry overviews including briefings of industry trends. Hoovers Online *(www.stockscreener.com)* offer excellent information on industries at their website. *Research* magazine *(www.researchmag.com)* offers helpful references to industry news, columns, and highlights.

Insurance

If you are paying for your own insurance, go to *www.ehealthinsurance.com*to determine if there is a less expensive plan to switch to. The website at *www.nmfn.com* will help you estimate your life span and need for life insurance based on your age, gender, lifestyle, and medical history.

International Investing

The Internet is rich in sources for information on foreign companies. Three websites in particular with useful information are *www.bankofny.com, wwwjpmorgan.com,* and *www.global-investor.com.* Also, FT Market Watch *(wwwftmarketwatch.com)* provides up-to-the minute news on offshore companies and foreign markets.

Investment Advice

The websites at *www.morningstar.com, www.kiplinger.com,* and *www.investools.com* will help you select stocks and mutual funds that meet your investment parameters. Shop around for the best certificate of deposit rates in your area at *www.bankrate.com.* To learn more about home loans, foreclosure prevention, and predatory lending, go to *www.loansafe.org.* Bankrate.com can find the best rates available in your area for motor vehicles.

Bank of America's website *(www.bankamerica.com)* offers a retirement center under the heading Achieve Your Goals on their main menu. It has several useful references for advice for retirees. Investor Home *(www.investorhome.com)* provides information about the investment process and how to bulletproof your portfolio.

Investment Associations

American Association of Individual Investors *(www.aaii.com)* offers a variety of valuable services to their members, including local chapter meetings in the major metropolitan areas.

The National Association of Investors Corporation (NAIC) is a national association with local chapters throughout the country. Their goal is to help investors develop a disciplined approach to successful investing. For more information, visit their website at *www.better-investing.org.*

Magazines

Business Week (www.businessweek.com) is available online to all of its subscribers.

Forbes (www.forbes. com) is available online and features articles on personal finance and investing.

Fortune (wwwfortune.com) includes special market reports as well as stock and fund quotes.

Kiplinger's (www.kiplinger.com) has a broader scope than many of its competitors. Instead of talking just about investing, *Kiplinger's* moves into other issues of personal business, such as credit card spending, loans, college tuition, and vacation planning. For subscription information, call 800-624-2946.

Newsweek (www.newsweek.com) not only covers the general news but also covers the latest news about the stock market. *SmartMoney* is the "*Wall Street Journal*" magazine of personal business" and it's excellent. For subscription information, call 800-444-4204 or visit their website at *www.smartmoney.com*.

Worth columnists, including Peter Lynch, are second to none, and the magazine's regular features are dynamite. For subscription information, call 800-777-1851 or go to *www.worth. com*. *Money* does an excellent job of keeping its readers informed about what's happening in the mutual fund market. For subscription information, visit their website at *www.money.com*.

Motor Vehicle Acquisition

For comprehensive car-buying information, go to *www.edmunds.com, www.autobytelcom,* and *www.carsmart.com*. To get an estimate of used car values, go to the Kelly Blue Book at *www.kbb.com,* Edmunds at *www.cdmunds.com,* or eAuto at *www.eauto.com*. If you are interested in purchasing a used vehicle, check out:

Trader Online *(www.traderonline.com)*
 Kelley Blue Book's Classifieds *(www.kbb.com)*
 Online Auto *(www.onlineauto.com)*
Auto Web Interactive *(www.autoweb.com)*.

If you are interested in purchasing a new vehicle, check out *www.autosite.com* to find dealer invoice prices or find out about the maintenance records on cars that interest you.

Mutual Fund Companies and Brokers

Charles Schwab *(www.schwab.com)*
Fidelity Investments *(www.jidelity.com)*
T. Rowe Price *(www.troweprice.com)*
Vanguard Group *(www.vanguard.com)*

Mutual Funds

There are almost as many mutual funds to choose from as there are stocks. The following websites will help you find the best ones out there:

CBS Market Watch *(www.marketwatch.com)* provides articles, news, and market data on funds.

MaxFunds *(www.maxfunds.com)* specializes in offering news and statistics on small and little-known funds.

Morningstar *(www.morningstar.com)* is a premier site providing all kinds of information about mutual funds.

Fidelity *(wwwjidelity.com)* offers direct purchase plans for its funds.

Janus *(www.janus. com)* has a family of no-load funds that you can purchase or apply for online.

T. Rowe Price *(www.troweprice.com)* offers direct purchase plans for its funds.

Vanguard *(www.vanguard.com)* has more than eighty funds that you can purchase directly from the company.

News Online

One of the biggest advantages of getting your news online is that you can go to the specific news sector (e.g., Market Watch) without having to thumb through a bunch of paper to get there. Here are several excellent sites to try:

ABC News *(www.abcnews.com)* features business and industry news and market commentary.

Bloomberg Personal Finance *(www.bloomberg.com)* is loaded with timely business news, data, and an analysis of the market.

News Page *(www.newspage.com)* allows you to customize daily news abstracts that it sends to your e-mail address.

Newspapers

Financial newspapers are still a way of life in the stock market's paper-oriented world, although some of them are beginning to make the migration over to the online sector. Here's a rundown of several excellent papers that are out there:

The *Financial Times (wwwft.com)* provides special reports on the market and the different industry sectors.

Investor's Business Daily is a great financial newspaper that publishes important information to help determine the value of a stock. For subscription information, call 800-831-2525 or visit their website at *www.investors.com.*

The *New York Times (www.nytimes.com)* provides a business section that includes quotes and charts, a portfolio management tool, and breaking business news.

USA Today (www.usatoday.com) features a money section that includes investment articles and news, economic information, and information on industry groups.

The *Wall Street Journal* is the "Big Kahuna" among investment newspapers, although its authority isn't as unquestioned as it used to be. For subscription information, call 800-778-0840 or visit their website at *www.wsj.com.*

Portfolio Management

There are several portfolio management tools that you can use to manage your portfolio. Check out the following websites:

Morningstar (*www.morningstar.com*) provides a portfolio setup menu that is easy to use.

Quicken *(www.quicken.com)* offers a variety of financial tools including an excellent portfolio-management program.

Microsoft (*www.money.msn.com)* offers a wealth of financial data.

Professional Advice

The following websites will provide you with access to professional advisors:

www.napfa.org
www.fpanet.org
www.aicpa.org

Quotes (Stocks and Mutual Funds)

American Stock Exchange (*www.amex.com)* offers quoting services on their website for stocks that are traded on its exchange.

Microsoft Investor (*www.investor.msn.com)* offers a free stock ticker that you can personalize along with portfolio-tracking tools.

The National Association of Securities Dealers *(www. nasdaq.com)* offers quoting services on their website for stocks that are traded on its exchange.

The New York Stock Exchange *(www.nyse.com)* offers quoting services on their website for stocks that are traded on its exchange.

PC Quote *(www.pcquote.com)* offers current stock prices, portfolio tracker, company profiles, and broker recommendations.

Business Week (www.businessweek.com/investor) features applicable information for researching investment opportunities.

Real Estate

Cost-of-living and moving calculators are available at *http://cgi.money.cnn.com/tools*. To calculate mortgage rates and review *Money* magazine articles on real estate, go to *www.usatoday.comlmoney*. The following websites will provide you with additional information on real estate:

www.bankrate.com
www.realestate.msn.com
www.craigslist.com
www.wheretoretire.com

Reducing Expenses

The following websites will provide you with information about how to reduce expenses:

www.carpoolworld.com
www.erideshares.com
www.campusbookretals.com
www.chegg.com
www.billshrink.com
www.energystar.gov

Retirement Planning

Charles Schwab's website will help you develop a retirement plan with their online calculators, tools, and advice at *www.schwab.com* (click on Advice & Retirement at the top of the menu).
Quicken offers a software product called Will Maker that is available at several computer stores and online at *www.nolo.com.* A retirement budget worksheet is available at *wwwjidelity.com* when you select the Retirement & Guidance option in their main menu.

A retirement calculator can be accessed at *www.usnews.com* when you select the Retirement sub-menu that is under their Money &

Business main menu. If you are interested in getting an annuity quote, go to *www.immediateannuities.com*. The following websites will provide you with additional information on retirement planning:

www.flexibleretirementPlanner.com
www.immediateannuities.com
www.quicken.com/retirment/planner
www.kinplinger.com
www.smartmoney.com
www.money.com
www.schwab.com
60 Plus Association at *www.60plus.org*
American Association of Retired People at *www.aarp.org*
Fifty Plus at *www.fifty-plus.net*
Grand Times at *www.grandtimes.com*
Hoover's Online *(www.stockscreener.com)* provides a special module for retirement planning.
Information Seniors at *www.infoseniors.com*

Reverse Mortgages

The following websites will provide you with additional information about reverse mortgages:

www.aarp.com
www.revmort.com/nrmla

Savings Programs

For steps to take to save money, go to *www.themoneykeys.com*. To determine if you are saving enough, go to *www.kiplinger.com*

Shopping and Selling

If you are shopping for an item or selling a household item that would be difficult to get an appraisal on, see what similar items are selling for in the classified advertisements or on *www.ebay.com, www.netmarket.com,* or *www.craigslist.com.* Yellow Page listings are available at *http://search.bigfoot.com* or *www.switchboard.com.* The following websites will provide you with additional information on shopping and buying on the internet:

www.bluefly.com
www.yoox.com

Stock and Mutual Fund Market Timing

The following websites will provide you with additional information on timing the stock and mutual fund markets:

www.schwab.com
www.trowprice.com
vanguard.com
www.fidelity.com
www.fundalarm.com
www.timingthemarket.net
www.stockcharts.com
www.vectorvest.com

Stock Evaluation Programs

Finding out what stock analysts are saying about a stock that you're considering can help you determine if it's the right time to buy. Here are several sites that will get you the information you need:

VectorVest *(www.vectorvest.com)* offers free reports showing what your stocks are really worth, how safe they are, and when to buy, sell, or hold. It's one of the best analyst's sites on the Internet.

S&P Advisor Insight *(www.advisorinsight.com)* allows you to review Standard & Poor's reports for major stocks.

Zacks Investment Research *(www.zacks.com)* reports on what analysts are saying about most of the stocks on the U.S. exchanges.

Stock Exchanges

The American, NASDAQ and New York Stock Exchanges offer a wide variety of investment features that may appeal to you.

American Stock Exchange *(www.amex.com)*.

The National Association of Securities Dealers *(www. nasdaq.com)*.

The New York Stock Exchange *(www.nyse.com)*.

Taxes

For tax deductions, go to *www.bottomlinesecrets.comlextra*. For tax preparation ideas, go to *http://tax.yahoo.comlchecklist.html*.

Travel Websites

www.expedia.com
www.travelocity.com
www.besifares.com
www.budgettravel.com

Web Search Engines

Alta Vista: *www.altavista.com*
Google: *www.google.com*
HotBot: *www.hotbot.com*
Lycos: *uruno.lycos.com*
Yahoo!: *www.yahoo.com*

About the Author & Testimonials

David Rye earned an MBA with honors from Seattle University, and is president of Western Publications. He writes and publishes personal finance books from his Goodyear, Arizona office. His award-winning books include *250 Questions You Need To Ask Before You Retire, Starting Up*, and *1001 Way to Inspire Yourself.*

"David's books are perfect for boomers who are about to retire and are thinking about starting up their own business … and make some extra money … in a format that's fun to read."
    Dr. T.K. Nelsen, Stanford University

"A great book in a writing style that is highly interactive where each chapter challenges to reader to expand their role in retirement … you'll learn how you can retire in \$tyle."
    Dale Moser, President and CEO, Niwot Technology, Inc.

"A hands-on book that dramatically illustrates how anyone can make money after they retire … and have fun doing it."
    Mark Kruger, Ph.D., Creative Thinking Seminars

"… adds an element of real world reality to the retirement process that is truly unique and refreshing."
    A.J. Osorio, President, Llanos Publishing